PROMPTINGS
Your Inner Guide to
Making a Difference

KODY BATEMAN

EAGLEONE

PUBLISHING

Promptings: Your Inner Guide to Making a Difference, first paperback edition ©2010, first hardcover edition ©2009 Kody Bateman. Published and distributed in the United States by Eagle One Publishing, LLC, www.eagleonepublishing.com, www. promptingsbook.com. SendOutCards® is a registered trademark of Send Out Cards, LLC, Salt Lake City, Utah. Editor: Melody Marler Forshée, Eagle One Publishing, LLC.

For information about special discounts for bulk purchases, contact Eagle One Publishing, info@eagleonepublishing.com.

ISBN: 978-0-9842703-6-1

Printed in the United States of America

EAGLE ONE

PUBLISHING

This book is dedicated to the inner voice within you—the voice that tells you who you are and celebrates your genius within.
Listen to your voice and make the difference that only you can make.

PRAISE FOR *PROMPTINGS*

"Kody shares his heart in a story that allows the reader to experience his journey of divine promptings and life's lessons along with the imprints left of those who have mentored and touched his life. His love for humanity shows that 'love comes in colors too' and that each one of us have the power to love."

LINDA CLEMONS, CEO, SISTERPRENEUR® INC.

"I commend Kody Bateman for bringing into our awareness the need to heed the 'promptings' we receive in life. His book, *Promptings: Your Inner Guide to Making a Difference,* calls us to consciously consider who we are, what we are doing and how we are connected to each other. Using his voice and his personal experiences to share what is possible, he provides readers with the insight and the inclination to hear and respond to life's quiet directions."

STEDMAN GRAHAM, BEST-SELLING AUTHOR, *YOU CAN MAKE IT HAPPEN* AND *DIVERSITY: LEADERS NOT LABELS*

"There are very few people who can successfully teach, through word and song, the universal principle of finding one's true purpose. Kody Bateman has done it. His message and music will change your life!"

THURL BAILEY, INSPIRATIONAL SPEAKER, SINGER-SONGWRITER, FORMER NBA PLAYER

"What an amazing way of looking at the world. *Promptings* is a celebration of life. Kody's perspective has empowered a team of people to grow a company from $200,000 to $50 million in record time. But the best part is that his way is effortless, and it feels great. Trying harder isn't always the answer. Miracles happen when you act on your promptings."

JORDAN ADLER, AUTHOR, *BEACH MONEY*

"After speaking with Kody for five minutes, he inspired me to renew a broken relationship and be at peace. This book is unlike any other. After reading it, you know it is sincere and straight from the heart. It causes you to reflect, but most importantly, Promptings will inspire and launch you into a new chapter of your life, even after major setbacks. Kody has given a new definition to the word 'prompting.' "

LES BROWN, MOTIVATIONAL SPEAKER, BEST-SELLING AUTHOR

"Wow, I can't believe Kody Bateman wrote a book about me! Seriously, everything I've ever been successful at throughout my entire life has been a manifestation of Kody's message. There is no question that *Promptings* unlocks the door to success in anything you do. This is a must-read for any person striving to become more than they are today. Awesome!"

TOMMY WYATT, CO-AUTHOR, *APPRECIATION MARKETING*

CONTENTS

INTRODUCTION

Promptings made me reflect on my life. As I read through Kody's book, my memory played back the numerous times I had a nudge, a small voice speaking from within, a coincidence, something that told me to stop and move in a different direction. Sometimes I listened and acted; many times I didn't. I asked myself, what would my life be if I let my tragedies and setbacks turn into stepping stones and inspiration for the rest of the world? And then I became sad.

Most people who look at my career would say, "Les Brown, you've inspired the masses." Well, the truth is, I haven't done much at all. See, I've had some lessons I was too embarrassed to share. I'll bet you have too. I've had some tragic losses that made me curl up in my bed and smother my tears in a pillow. I know you've had the same experience. In fact, I've laid down many nights hoping to never see the sunlight again, and I still woke up. To my surprise, life still welcomed me, with a few black eyes and bruises, of course, but I was still here.

More importantly, after thinking about my stumbling blocks, I was sad to have wasted so much time being depressed. I wasted so much of my energy complaining, talking to anyone who would listen about my "terrible life" and looking at all of the closed doors; I never took the time to acknowledge the open doors.

I often say, "When things go wrong, don't go with them." Did my setbacks mean I was a failure? No, but rejecting my promptings meant I was throwing in the towel on myself. Kody says it best with the phrase he has coined, "old tennis balls." I was the dog who picked up the old, more comfortable, used ball. I had new opportunities that I simply ignored by hanging on to unimportant stuff—you know, the negative conversations in your head talking you out of pursuing more, pursuing your dreams.

What I love about Kody Bateman and *Promptings* is his transparency and tenacity, his propensity to turn lemons into lemonade. Most of us have experienced adversity. He chose to react to adversity by stimulating new growth. This book tells you exactly what he did and how you can do it. The concept is quite simple: Watch successful people and do what they do. And observe unsuccessful people and do the exact opposite. Kody has presented a blueprint for success in many areas—emotional healing, forgiveness, success coaching, business training, and so much more.

Make your promptings matter. And I don't mean being prompted to curse someone out, even though I've been there too! Let your misfortune prompt you to change lives, express appreciation, start a business—and lead a life that matters.

I admire Kody's brilliance with his message to use your promptings to help others. I urge you to look at your life and be grateful for the darker days. Reflect and think about how your story can make a difference in the lives of others. You're not the only one dealing with job loss, family problems, addiction, a failed business—but reacting positively to your experiences could renew your life.

I firmly believe everyone has a story to tell. I call it your Power Voice. Discover it and change lives. Get out of your head and into your greatness, and let your promptings promote greatness and inspiration across the globe.

LES BROWN, MOTIVATIONAL SPEAKER
AND BEST-SELLING AUTHOR

"You cannot do a kindness too soon, for you never know how soon it will be too late."

RALPH WALDO EMERSON

CHAPTER 1

My Brother Kris

In 1989 I was hired by an advertising agency in New York City. I had just graduated from college and completed an advertising internship. My career was getting off to a great start, and I was excited.

I was ready to move from my home in Salt Lake City to the vast unknown in the big city. My wife and I and our one-year-old daughter prepared for our journey. It came time to say our farewells to family and friends, and then we jumped in the car to leave. Like it was yesterday, I remember getting in our car and looking out at the field next to my parents' house. My brother, Kris, was moving some vehicles around. At that moment I had a prompting that I needed to slow down and take the time to run over and give my big brother a hug and say goodbye. I ignored that prompting. We jumped in the car, honked, waved and drove away.

Two months later, in a small apartment in New Jersey, we received a phone call in the middle of the night. My mother tearfully let me know that my brother Kris had been killed earlier that day. She told me Kris, who worked as an electrician, had been called to fix some lights at a tennis court. He climbed up a metal pole that had a pulley system at the top. The pulley system had a metal cable Kris pulled on to bring the lights over the tennis court toward him. As he was pulling on this cable, it broke and swung over his head, connecting with a 7,200-volt power line behind him. He was electrocuted and fell some twenty feet to his death. Later in the day, a girl playing tennis went to retrieve a ball and found my brother's body behind some bushes. When my mother finished the story we said our goodbyes, and I was left to ponder the news I had just received. The only thing I could think of was that I had ignored a prompting to say goodbye to my brother Kris.

That was a defining moment in my life. I made a promise to my brother that night that I would never ignore a prompting again. I also promised that I would help as many people as I could to act on their promptings to reach out to others. This moment changed my life forever. I immediately began my journey to not only learn the power of promptings, but to find ways to make it simple for people to act on them.

We flew home for the funeral, and, as you would expect, it was a very difficult time for my family. Kris was only twenty-nine years old and left a young widow and three small children. I remember going to his home to visit his young family. It was a new home, and the yard had not been put in yet. Kris was planning to get started on the yard that weekend.

I remember standing in their front room, looking out the window. What I saw next was another defining moment for me. All of a sudden, eight or nine trucks pulled up in front of their home, and fathers and sons started piling out of those vehicles. Picks and shovels in hand, they marched into the yard. More trucks pulled up with loads of topsoil, loads of sod, sprinkler pipe, wood for a fence, and parts for a swing set and playground. Within four hours this small army of concerned people had installed the entire front and back yard, fence, sprinklers, grass, swing set, sandbox, and all. Our family was filled with emotion.

No words could have ever been spoken to comfort our family the way this enormous act of kindness did.

I walked outside and asked who had put this whole thing together. I was guided to a young man about twenty-five years old. I asked him what gave him the idea to do this incredible act.

He said, "Kody, you see all these people working in your brother's yard? Your brother helped almost every one of us put our yards in." He was very saddened by the news of my brother's death, but when driving out of the neighborhood that morning, he looked at my brother's home and noticed the yard had not been put in yet. And he had a *prompting* that come hell or high water, before the sun set over the west mountains that night, that yard would be completed.

It's amazing to me that this young man used the same word: *prompting*. I ignored a prompting and lost a brother. I then witnessed the result of acting upon a prompting—a prompting that delivered an army of people to a young widow's yard and springboarded the healing process of an entire family.

I will never forget the powerful impact this experience had on my life. I received the message loud and clear that my mission in life was to act on my promptings and help others do the same.

Since that time I have been on a life journey learning the enormous value of promptings in our lives. I have learned that promptings will guide you to your genius within. I have learned that promptings are not to be analyzed; they are to be acted upon. And I have learned there are two primary types of promptings: The first is the inner prompting that tells you who you are; the second is the outer prompting that tells you what to do with who you are.

The inner prompting is that voice within that only you can hear. We have all heard our own song in our hearts. At some point in our lives we have all connected with our own uniqueness. You may or may not be currently blessed with a clear direction from your inner promptings. That inner voice may currently be difficult to hear or it may be very clear. Either way, by acting on your outer promptings you will strengthen that inner voice, and it will guide you to what you were destined to be. Promptings do guide you to your genius within.

The more we act on these promptings, the bigger difference we make in the world. People crave the feelings of being appreciated, accepted, and loved. We are all given promptings or impressions to deliver those very things to the people in our lives. The more we act on these promptings, the more in tune we become, and the promptings become stronger and clearer. We even receive them more frequently.

I remember an experience as a fourteen-year-old boy when my inner voice or inner promptings began to speak clearly to me. Someone gave me the book *How to Win Friends and Influence People* by Dale Carnegie. This was the first book that I actually read cover to cover. I loved that book. I underlined key points and wrote notes on the margins of its pages. When I finished that book I quickly discovered there were many more books like it. The next book I read was *The Power of Positive Thinking* by Dr. Norman Vincent Peale. I then started reading all the books written by Og Mandino. To this day he is my favorite author.

I started receiving inner promptings that told me I should do what these authors were doing. I should share the message of positive thinking. I should share stories of inspiration, I should help others build self-esteem, I should teach the message of hope, and I should write words that uplift and encourage people to reach their potential. I was blessed with the gift of happiness. I always believed anything was possible and I couldn't understand why other people didn't think that way. These books nourished that passion within and helped me recognize my inner promptings. I began to listen and got really excited about my future.

At the time I did not know exactly what my message would be, but I knew I was destined to make a difference with a positive message to the world. I learned that these authors also gave speeches. I remember as a teenager listening to a cassette tape where a motivational speaker was telling stories. He made me laugh, he made me think, and he even made me cry. I thought this was the coolest thing I had ever heard.

My inner promptings were saying I would grow up and carry a message through writing and the spoken word. Again I did not know what the message would be, but I did know that I would be guided to it. How did I know that? My inner promptings told me so.

For the next nine years I simply grew up. I finished high school, served a church mission, and went to college. I excelled in any class where writing was required. I loved my psychology and sociology classes because I felt they were guiding me to the message I would deliver. I remember mapping out theories and philosophies on large scrolls of paper, and I would lose track of time while doing it. During all of this I continued to read personal development books.

I graduated from college, completed a New York City internship and moved my wife and daughter to New Jersey. I remember walking through the streets of New York City and passing a bookstore. I saw a new book release in the window titled *Unlimited Power* by Anthony Robbins. I immediately bought that book and was inspired by it. I remember thinking, *This Robbins guy is amazing. He is living my dream.*

I vividly remember a sunny afternoon in Hackensack, New Jersey. My wife was doing some shopping, and I was reading this Tony Robbins book in the car. Like always, I had my pen in hand, underlining key phrases and writing notes and loving every minute of it. I was still searching for my unique message, and I knew I was getting close.

It was only a few days later that I received the phone call from my mother, telling me my brother Kris had been killed. I was left to ponder the fact that I had ignored a prompting to say goodbye to him when we moved.

You know the rest of the story. We flew home for the funeral, and I was given the message I was supposed to deliver to the world. The message I had searched for was packaged up in one little word: *promptings*. I learned how important it was to act on the outer promptings when they come your way—that simple thought that tells you to reach out in kindness to others.

I made a promise to my brother Kris that I would act on those, and I immediately made it a habit to do so. I was amazed how quickly they transformed my life, guiding me to where I was supposed to go, who I was supposed to meet, what I was supposed to do. The more I acted on those outer promptings, the more clear the inner promptings became. I was excited because I knew how powerful this simple message was. I knew how much it could help me and others throughout the world. Nine years of searching for my message came together with the passing of my brother, and I knew exactly what I would be doing with the rest of my life.

You may be thinking this all sounds so dramatic. That's because it is. When you live a life with passion, it is dramatic. It's exciting. It's fun.

You may be thinking I sure thought a lot of myself to believe I actually would find a message that would change the world. Well, I did think a lot of myself, and I did find that message. That belief came from a strong self-image, and everyone has the capacity to acquire that in their lives.

Every person reading this book has uniqueness in them. There are things in this world only you can do. There are people that, at certain times, only you can reach. There is genius within you that only you have. I do think a lot of myself, and it's time you start doing the same. We were all destined for greatness, and anything less than that is an excuse. I choose not to live with excuses; I live with possibilities. I believe anything is possible if you follow your own inner promptings and have the courage to allow them to guide you. I believe your inner promptings define who you are and your outer promptings allow you to change the world with who you are.

"With the right attitude human beings can move mountains. With the wrong attitude they can be crushed by the smallest grain of sand."

JIM ROHN

"Only a person with a best seller mind can write best sellers."

ALDOUS LEONARD HUXLEY

CHAPTER 2

Old Tennis Balls: Excuses and Limiting Beliefs

I have a black lab named Gus. He is an incredible dog. No matter what, Gus is always happy to see me. He is anxious to play and have a good time with anyone willing to take the time. Dogs teach us the most important lesson about happy living. They love us unconditionally, and they expect very little in return. They will play with you, cuddle with you, and even sense when something might be wrong.

A few years ago I took my son Sawyer and Gus out to the desert for some Saturday fun. We took the four-wheelers and planned to ride while Gus ran along with us. I remember arriving at our riding spot, getting out of the truck, letting Gus out of his riding kennel, and lowering the gate to our four-wheeler trailer. That's it. The next thing I knew it was four hours later, and I was sitting on the floor of the family room in my home. To this day I remember nothing that took place during that four hours. Luckily my son was there to witness what happened, and he ended up saving my life. We had unloaded the machines, put on our riding gear, and took off on a trail that we often rode.

Less than five minutes into the ride I flipped my machine and landed on my head. I was knocked out, even though I was wearing a helmet. When my son found me I was lying on the ground next to my overturned machine, and Gus was laying right next to me with his head resting on my chest.

For those of you who know the nature of Labrador retrievers, they are known for running free in open spaces. They don't stop for much of anything. Gus knew something was wrong, and he stayed there to protect me. Sawyer was only ten years old at the time. He managed to track down some dirt bike riders and wave them over to help. Those riders got me back to our truck, loaded our machines, put Gus in his riding kennel, and drove us forty miles back to our home. Apparently I was conscious on the ride home and having discussions with these guys, but I don't remember anything until I was sitting on my living room floor. My wife took me to the emergency room to get checked out. While sitting on the doctor's table, I began gasping for air. I had bruised my sternum, punctured a lung, and had a concussion.

The doctor insisted I stay the night in the hospital so the staff could keep a close watch on me. When it came time for everyone to leave for the night, my ten-year-old son Sawyer refused to leave my side. He said our dog Gus stayed by his dad's side, so he could too. I will never forget that moment. Not only was it a special bonding moment between a father and son, but it was a teaching moment as well. Our dog Gus taught a ten-year-old boy what it means to care for someone.

Dogs are amazing because they can be incredibly focused on things they want, but they will always be there to give us humans what we want: to be loved and accepted. Dogs give us that unconditionally, and they always find time to run off and find their hidden treats and treasures in the back yard. This is called balance, a balance between their own desires and the needs of others around them.

Well, as with most black Labs, Gus loves to play fetch. I love to walk into the back yard bouncing a tennis ball. When Gus notices that ball, he goes crazy. He knows if I am bouncing a tennis ball in front of him, it won't be long before I throw it out in the yard for him to go fetch. He will look up with his happy eyes, furiously wag his tail back and forth and impatiently wait for the fun to begin.

When I throw that tennis ball, Gus takes off on a dead run and snatches it in his mouth as fast as he can. He always runs right back to me with the prize. When he gets back to me, he does not like to let go of that ball. In fact, I have to pry it out of his mouth. Usually when I do, he has managed to slobber all over it. But I take that grimy ball and throw it out in the yard again, where it usually lands in dirt. Most of you know that when a slobbery ball rolls in the dirt, the dirt stays on the ball. So now it's grimy, slobbery, and dirty. Gus doesn't care. He will snatch that ball up in his mouth and come running back to me for more.

By this time in the game I always like to bring out another shiny new tennis ball. Gus will come back with the old grimy ball in his mouth and see that I have a new one. He is so excited at the possibility of getting his jaws around that new ball. As I bounce it in front of him, he watches while keeping the old grimy ball in his mouth. When I finally throw that ball out in the yard, he will run out to it as fast as he can. But when he gets to the ball he will stop, look down at the new ball, look back at me, look back down at the new ball, and wonder what to do. You see, he refuses to let go of the old tennis ball, so he can't figure out how to pick up the new one. In his confusion he will lie down next to the new ball—and the game is over.

Now before you start calling Gus crazy or dumb, I challenge you to analyze your own life. How often do we see new opportunities come our way, get excited about those opportunities, but find ourselves unable to take advantage because we have some old tennis ball—or an old, limiting belief—we are hanging onto?

WHAT ARE THE OLD TENNIS BALLS YOU ARE HANGING ONTO?

What are the old tennis balls keeping you from living your full potential? The old tennis balls in our life show up as excuses, limiting beliefs, and plain old stinking thinking—things like, "I'm too old to start something new," "I don't deserve it," "I'm not good at new technology," "I don't know the right people," "I can't get a break because things are too political," "I didn't get in on the ground floor," "I'm not smart enough," "I don't have the time," "It takes money to make money," "People are out to get me," "I can't trust anyone," "It wasn't meant to be," or the best one of all, "I must accept my fate!"

Excuse me. I need to stop writing for a second so I can go take a shower. I feel dirty after writing that last paragraph. That is some of the dirtiest language anyone can think, let alone write. Those things are nothing more than old dirty, grimy, slimy, ugly tennis balls. If we are hanging on to them, we cannot accept, let alone pick up, the new ones thrown out to us. It seems silly that we hang on to the old tennis balls, the limiting beliefs that dramatically hold us back. Why do we do it, and where did those grimy tennis balls come from?

Somewhere along the line we started allowing excuses and limiting beliefs to enter our subconscious minds. It started showing up **in the language we use every day.** We started to say we had problems instead of challenges. We started to consistently use words like can't, try, don't, no, never, realistic, and any other limiting word that created grimy, ugly tennis balls. The more we used this language the more we subconsciously suffered. This didn't happen overnight. It took years, and slowly but surely we started heading our mindset in the wrong direction.

So how do we turn this around? How do we change this kind of thinking? I suggest we go back to our dogs, who teach us valuable lessons about life. The only way I can get Gus to let go of the old grimy tennis ball in his mouth is to throw the new one over and over and over again. If I keep doing this, eventually he will drop the old tennis ball and pick up the new one. So how do we create and throw ourselves the new tennis balls? We do it the same way we created the old ones but at a faster, more creative and productive way.

NEW TENNIS BALLS!

We simply create the statements we desire in present tense and start throwing those messages to ourselves over and over again. Most of us have heard of affirmations or goals or mission statements. You keep hearing about them because they work. I like to call them "I am" statements. I call them that because if each statement begins with the words "I am," you ensure the statement is in present tense. Your subconscious mind does not know the difference between what is real or imagined, so if you state in present tense the things you desire, your subconscious mind says, "OK." It accepts whatever you send it as if it already exists.

If you don't believe this, think of all the negative statements you have been sending to yourself—many times without even knowing it. As an example, if you have been saying, "I can't afford it," guess what? You are right. Your subconscious mind says, "OK," and it delivers exactly what you have been sending it. You can't afford it. Without even knowing it, you have been throwing out an "I am" statement that says, "I can't afford it." The problem is obvious. That is a negative statement. It created a negative belief, and it produced a negative result. In my own life I replaced this statement with many new ones, statements like, "I am attracting wealth in abundance," "I am financially independent and free," and "I am a money magnet." Amazing things have happened in my financial life since I started throwing these new statements to my subconscious mind over and over and over again. In addition I make a point to get rid of any negative language in my life. You will never hear me say, "I can't afford it." I will say things like, "I choose not to spend my money on that at this time." See the difference? This keeps a positive message flowing to your subconscious mind in terms of money. These principles apply to any area in your life.

THE "I AM" STATEMENT IS WHO YOU ARE

Now let me fill you in on a little secret: The "I am" statements you create are your inner promptings speaking to you. Your "I am" statements are who you are. The power of the "I am" statements is that you already are the things you include on the statement. Remember, the inner prompting is who you are, and the outer prompting is what you do with who you are.

My inner promptings told me I would have a positive message to share with the world. My brother's death produced a promise I made to my brother that I would act on my promptings to reach out in kindness to myself and others, and that I would help others do the same. That promise led me to create a business with a service that helps people act on their promptings.

THE CHALLENGES OF A NEW BUSINESS VENTURE

Any time you start a business with a new concept and a new technology, you will face your share of challenges. To help people act on their promptings we created a greeting card and gift service that works over the Internet. The concept is simple: A person receives a prompting to thank someone, and they need a quick way to act on that prompting before they lose it. We created a service where you go online to choose a greeting card from an online catalog or create your own from pictures you took with your digital camera. Type a message on the inside—you can even create your own handwriting font so it looks like you handwrote the message—add a gift to go with the greeting card, push send, and you are done. Our service receives your order, prints your card, stuffs it in an envelope, applies a first-class stamp, and puts it in the mail for you. If you added a gift, we put the card with the gift and send the package out the very next day. Great idea, right? Excellent idea, but it was a new idea. It required a shift in the habits of our potential consumer. We needed to educate consumers on how to send these cards. More importantly, we needed to remind them why they needed to send these cards.

It's challenging enough to start a time-tested traditional business. When you add all the components we just mentioned, it becomes a monumental task. My wife and I invested everything we had into this project. We had already been successful building a business, and we sold out to some partners so we could pursue this project full time. We went from a comfortable lifestyle back to starting all over again. We brought on partners, raised additional funds through private investors, and worked day and night to make this happen.

To make this work we needed to educate the consumer on how to send a card. We also needed a way to share the inspirational "why" behind acting on promptings. The best way to do this was through a network-marketing business model. This allowed us to create a large group of independent representatives who would sit down at a computer and show a new person how to send a card, add a picture to a card, create group lists, and send cards to numerous people at once; later, the representatives could invite them to an inspirational seminar where they could learn the "why" behind acting on promptings and how this service would dramatically improve their business, their relationships, and their personal lives.

The challenge was nobody had ever sold a greeting card and gift service through network marketing. We were the pioneers. We paved our own roads before we could travel on them. This required a tremendous amount of trial and error. We had to find the right compensation structure for our independent representatives and offer our product and service at an affordable price. In fact, it was always our goal to offer a greeting card under market value because price was one reason why people did not always act on their promptings by sending a greeting card.

We needed to make it convenient, to never let customers forget birthdays and special occasions, to give them a way to send an unexpected greeting card daily, and to do it at a price most people could afford. We also needed to provide an opportunity where an independent representative was motivated to continually show the service to others. This was not an easy task. We spent a tremendous amount of money, effort, time, sweat, and tears to get this thing right. There were times in the early stages where we had more money going out than we had coming in. There were days when personal credit cards and lines of credit were used to meet payrolls and commissions. As with most start-up ventures, we faced some very challenging times.

HOW DID WE TURN IT AROUND?

At our lowest point I remember getting on a plane and flying to San Antonio, Texas. I went there to meet with a business associate and friend who was in the personal-development distribution business. I visited his warehouse where he stored thousands of books, videos, and tapes that would be distributed all over the world. I remember walking down an isle in his warehouse and seeing a book titled *Excuse Me,*

Your Life is Waiting by Lynn Grabhorn. My friend gave me that book, and I read it with pen in hand, doing what I always do with my books: I underlined and wrote notes throughout the pages. Though its message was nothing new, I loved the way Grabhorn wrote about simple Law of Attraction principles. Her words resonated with my heart and soul, and I was inspired by her approach. She talked about affirmations, as many such books do. Even though I had written affirmations in the past, she inspired me to do so again.

On the way back to the airport I stopped at a convenience store and bought a packet of index cards. It cost me $1.09. I got on the airplane, lowered the tray from the seat in front of me, and wrote down my affirmations. As you know, I call them "I am" statements, and I would like to share those statements with you. Keep in mind, I wrote these at a low point in my life. It was time for me to remind myself who I really was. It was time to celebrate Kody Bateman in my own mind. Here are the statements I wrote:

> *I am an inspirational writer*
> *I am an exceptional speaker and trainer*
> *I am a master facilitator*
> *I inspire people to live their potential*
> *I encourage people to send out their best*
> *I challenge people to make a difference*
> *I train, teach, and motivate people to build wealth*
> *I am a humorous and happy presenter*
> *I am passionate and enthusiastic*
> *I am speaking to sold-out seminars nationwide*
> *I am a best-selling author and speaker*
> *We are changing the world with a billion-dollar greeting card and gift enterprise*

> *We are reaching millions of people with SOC*
> *I am helping people become senders of cards*
> *I am attracting the right people into my business*
> *I am attracting wealth in abundance*
> *I am making $$$$$ per month*
> *I am financially independent and free*
> *I am enjoying a net worth of $$$$$*
> *I am keeping $1,000 cash in my money clip*
> *We are enjoying our new dream home*
> *We are enjoying a romantic, passionate, and happy*
> *marriage*
> *I am toned, strong, and in great shape*
> *I am spiritually in tune*
> *I am Kody B. The master MC*

This is who I really am. This is what my inner promptings were saying to me.

Now, at the time of writing these statements most people would say that none of those things were real because none of them had happened yet. I am here to tell you if you think that way, you are wrong. The stories you create in your mind are the stories that become your life. Every accomplishment and every possibility begins within, and the more real you treat those things, the faster you manifest them in your life.

After I wrote those statements I got off that airplane in my hometown, and things immediately started to happen. I believed those statements were already real, and I began to integrate them into my life at a rapid pace. One of the statements says, "I am attracting the right people into my business."

Two weeks after writing that statement, I received a phone call from a guy named DeMarr Zimmerman. At the time he was one of my newest business associates. He set up a three-way phone call with me and a gentleman by the name of Jordan Adler. DeMarr and Jordan worked with me to formulate a new compensation structure that would richly benefit the future of SOC. This is something my partners and I would never have been able to come up with on our own. Today both of those gentlemen are top income-earners in our business, and they are dear friends. They are responsible for bringing thousands of people into our business. *"I am attracting the right people into my business."*

I look back on that list of "I am" statements, and most of them have been manifested in my life. In fact, as I was writing this paragraph, I received a phone call from my wife telling me that we had been approved for the financing on our new dream home. If you recall, one of my statements was, "We are enjoying our new dream home."

We know who we are before anyone else does. The more real we treat those stories, the faster they become manifested in our lives.

The power of the "I am" is that you already are. Your inner promptings tell you who you are. You bring those promptings to life through the "I am" statements, and the more real you make them feel, the faster they manifest themselves into your life.

Your conscious mind and subconscious mind have to be in alignment. They have to be going after the same thing. In fact, whatever is in the subconscious mind is what happens no matter what. If your subconscious mind has been programmed to believe, as an example, that you are not deserving of a loving relationship, and your conscious mind is working hard to meet that special someone, what will happen? Chances are good that you won't meet that special someone or you will have a hard time getting a relationship to work out. Why? Because the thought that rests in your subconscious mind is what happens.

It's like my dog Gus. The first ball in his mouth is the one he hangs onto. The first dominant thought that we send to our subconscious mind is what we are hanging on to. If it is a *don't-want* thought, then it blocks us from getting what we *do want*. Now if you remember, the only way I could get Gus to drop the first ball was to throw the wanted ball over and over again until he finally dropped the unwanted ball.

This is the value of an "I am" statement. It states, in present tense, the things we do want. By stating these things over and over again, we are throwing the second ball to our subconscious mind. We are reprogramming our subconscious to accept the things we do want. Eventually this process will help us drop the first ball or the unwanted belief that we are hanging onto. What we *send out* to our subconscious mind is what we get back.

MASTERS OF THE "I AM" STATEMENT

Muhammed Ali was a master at the "I am" statement. He used to always say that he was the champ—even before he was the champ. He would predict the rounds that he would knock out his opponents, and he was almost always right. He used to always say, "I am the greatest in the world." He believed he was the champ and that he was the greatest before anyone else saw it. His inner promptings were telling him who he was. You will notice I did not explain who Muhammed Ali was when I told this story. Why? Because I didn't have to. Everyone knows who Muhammed Ali is. In fact, to this day he is the most widely recognized sports figure in the history of the world. Why? Muhammed Ali was the greatest.

Madonna is a master of the "I am" statement. She has always believed that she was a superstar—a master entertainer—even before she was known by many people. To this day she gathers her dancers and singers around in a circle and expresses a prayer of gratitude for the masterful way in which they performed their concert, and she does this before the concerts. Is it any wonder that Madonna is an entertainer that continually re-defines herself? In her early fifties, she is releasing new albums and performing world tours that are still in a league of their own.

At the time of this writing, Lebron James is a twenty-four-year-old basketball superstar playing in the NBA. He came straight out of high school to compete with the best basketball players in the world. He was named the Most Valuable Player in the 2008-2009 season. In an interview he was asked who his greatest sports heroes were while growing up. Here is his list:

Deion Sanders, football player

Emmitt Smith, football player

Anfernee "Penny" Hardaway, basketball player

Michael Jordan, basketball player

And get this:

Lebron James, basketball player

He put himself on the list of his sports heroes before anyone knew who he was. There was one person who knew, and that was Lebron.

There is an excellent book I recommend everyone should read, titled *The Power of Your Subconscious Mind* by Joseph Murphy. This book will help you understand just how powerful the "I am" statements are. We spend a great deal of time in our seminars teaching "I am" techniques that will help you *send out* your *do wants* to your subconscious mind. What we are doing is helping you to recreate your success blueprint that you have in your subconscious mind.

Writing "I am" statements, learning about them in interactive seminars, and practicing them is an ongoing personal-development technique. You become like a Muhammad Ali or Madonna or Lebron James. You get really good at them, and you begin to manifest your desires at a rapid pace.

It's like my dog Gus. I have been throwing those tennis balls in the backyard for years. Things are a bit different now with Gus. He has learned he does not have to hang onto the old ball. I usually only have to throw the new tennis ball out there once or maybe twice now before he drops the old and picks up the new. I encourage you to become a master of the "I am" statement. Learn from my dog Gus. Drop the unwanted stuff in your life and pick up those things you desire. Become the you that you were meant to be. Follow those inner promptings and believe in them.

"Whatever you think today becomes what you are tomorrow."

NAPOLEON HILL

"The biggest tragedy is the waste of human resources. The average person goes to his grave with his music still in him."

OLIVER WENDELL HOLMES

CHAPTER 3

The Power of the "I Am"

We had just completed one of our Treat'em Right seminars in Scottsdale, Arizona, and my lifelong friend Super Dave Smith and I went out to dinner. When we finished eating, we walked outside the restaurant, and sitting across the street was the most beautiful sports car I had ever seen. I didn't know what it was at first. Dave and I walked around the car and saw that it was an Aston Martin Vantage. A James Bond car. Right then and there I told Super Dave I was going to own a car just like that one.

When we flew home from that trip, I remember sitting on the airplane, reflecting back on reasons why it was important for me to own a car like that. I thought back on a trip I took with my family when I was twelve years old. My mom and dad loved to take us kids on road trips. Our whole family would pack into our big motor home and head out on the open highway. On this trip we drove from Salt Lake City to Los Angeles. I loved southern California, everything from Disneyland and Universal Studios to sunny beaches and palm trees.

I remember driving down the coast on Highway One. We were glued to the windows of that motor home, taking everything in. We stopped at an exotic car dealership in Malibu, California. They had shiny new Ferraris, Lamborghinis, and other European sports cars. We were not used to seeing cars like that in Utah in the late '70s. But we were in sunny southern California, and things were different there. Imagine me, a twelve-year-old kid with wide eyes and big dreams of flying down the road in one of these cool cars. I decided right then that someday I would own a fancy sports car like the ones we were looking at. When we left that dealership, we all piled back in the motor home. I told my older brothers I was going to own one of those cars when I grew up. They all started giving me a hard time, saying things like, "Kody, we are construction workers. We can't afford cars like that. You need to be more realistic."

I didn't like what they were saying, so I moved to the front of the motor home. There was a large double seat where the driver was. My dad was driving the motor home, and I sat right next to him on that double seat. I said, "Dad, someday I am going to own a car like the ones we just looked at." I will never forget what he said: "Son, if you want to own a car like that, I'm sure that you will." That was it.

❖

Fast forward close to thirty years. Dave and I walk out of a restaurant, and I see the fancy, exotic European sports car I wanted to buy. So what did I do? Well, I was teaching people the power of the "I am" statements, and I had written many that were now manifesting in my life. I simply sat down and wrote a statement that said, "I am enjoying my new Aston Martin V8 Vantage." We also taught the importance of visualizing your desires and writing the "why" behind what it is you desire. If you have a compelling enough "why," you can do anything. So in addition to writing the statement, I sent myself a greeting card.

I went to an Aston Martin dealership, took a digital picture of my dream car, and put it on the front of the card. On the inside left of the card I wrote:

> *I am enjoying my Aston Martin V8 Vantage.*
> *Why:*
> *This car is amazing, not because of how it looks or how much it costs. It's amazing because of how I feel when I drive it.*
> *I love the way it accelerates, the way it sets me back in the plush leather seats. I love the new car smell and the feel of the gas pedal and gear shifter. I love the feeling of abundance as I cruise down the road.*
> *The surround sound stereo places you in a state of feel-good.*
> *Traveling short distances or long distances is a treat.*

On the inside right I placed another digital image of me standing next to this car. When I completed building this greeting card, I sent it to myself in the mail. This was an amazingly powerful exercise. You will notice I used all of the senses as I sent a message to my subconscious mind. I stated, in present tense, that I was enjoying my new Aston Martin. I visualized it with pictures, and I wrote a statement of why that car was important to me. I mentioned how it smelled, how it felt sitting in the seats, how it sounded, what it was like to drive it, how it made me feel as I drove it. I brought that car to life on this greeting card I sent it to myself.

Now remember, your subconscious mind does not know the difference between what is real and imagined; my subconscious acted as if I had that car. I did this when our business was just getting started. At the time I was deeply in debt and did not have much money coming in. To make a long story short it was almost three years to the day of me sending myself this greeting card that I walked into an Aston Martin dealership in Denver, Colorado. I left that dealership a proud owner of an onyx black Aston Martin Vantage with light-tan leather interior.

Just one day before writing this story in this book, I drove that car to a family outing where most of my brothers and sisters were—the same ones who told me thirty years ago that I would probably never own a car like that. Their kids were taking my car for joy rides, and I was really enjoying the moment. I looked over at my dad, and he gave me that smirky smile he often does. We both remembered our conversation in the motor home so many years ago. Oh, by the way, the license plate on that car says "MY I AM." How appropriate.

"WE ARE ENJOYING OUR NEW DREAM HOME"

I have already mentioned that one of my "I am" statements says, "We are enjoying our new dream home." I did the same thing with this statement as I did with the car. We took a digital picture of our dream home and put it on the front of a "dream" greeting card. On the inside left of the card we loaded a digital picture of the view of the Wasatch Front mountains from the home.

On the inside right I wrote:

> *We are enjoying our new dream home.*
> *Why:*
> *Our home is a place of refuge. This is where our family builds memories and collects stories. This is where we enjoy the company of friends, associates, and extended family.*
>
> *This is a place of abundance. As we walk through this home, we enjoy the feel of luxury. We love the*

*smell of the furniture, the sound of the wood floors as
we walk from room to room. The kitchen is a place
for gourmet cooking, and it is a fun gathering place.
The library and den are a place for reflection—a
place to read, write, and meditate. The master suite
is a place where we can shut the doors and unwind
from the cares of the world. From the hot tubs and
steam rooms to the workout machines and sound
system, this is a place where we can live with good
habits and enjoy the process every day.*

You can see how I used all the senses and brought this home to life
by visualizing it with a dream greeting card.

Here is the interesting part of this story. The picture of the home
on this greeting card was taken in an affluent east-side neighborhood
known as Pepperwood in Salt Lake City, Utah. I used to show the
greeting card I created at our seminars all over the world. I would show
the pictures, read the message, and then, afterwards, I would go on
and explain more about the home. I would explain from the stage that
this was a 9,500-square-foot rambler with a nine-car shop and a pool
in the back yard. The only problem was this home in Pepperwood did
not have a nine-car shop or a pool in the backyard. In fact, the yard was
too small to have those things in the yard.

Two years after I had created the dream card and told the story
at forty-plus seminars, we found a completely different home on the
opposite side of town. This home was going into foreclosure, and we
wanted to purchase it. The home was caught in a bitter legal battle and
was blocked from going to auction. While looking at this home, we
would drive in the private gated lane and admire all the homes that
were there.

There was one occupied home in this neighborhood that we loved. One of the reasons is that it looked very similar to the home we had taken a picture of in Pepperwood. The difference was that this home was on a one-acre lot. It had a nine-car shop and a pool in the back-yard. Sound familiar?

Now here is the kicker: When the other home fell through, I received a phone call from the owner of the home that we really loved. You guessed it—they wanted to know if we would be interested in purchasing the home. And it gets even better: To purchase the home we needed to sell our home. It just so happens that the owners of our dream home wanted to downsize, and they offered to purchase our existing home.

The first thing I asked them when we walked through our dream home was, "What is the square footage?" Of course it was 9,500 square feet. And when you look out the back windows, we have the same view of the Wasatch Mountains as the one we took a picture of outside the original home.

KNOW WHAT YOU ARE SAYING BECAUSE THAT IS EXACTLY WHAT YOU WILL GET

Now listen, you can't make this stuff up. When you create an "I am" statement, visualize it, and state your compelling "why," your sub-conscious mind goes into action and delivers exactly what you tell it. You have all heard the saying, "You better be careful what you wish for because you just might get it." It's amazing how true those words are. When you write these statements, make sure you know what you are saying because that is exactly what you will get.

It is always helpful to do things as these stories suggest. Write your statements, visualize them as best as you can, state your "whys" using all the senses, and keep sending yourself this message over and over.

The dream greeting cards are an excellent way to use the latest technology to visualize your "I am" statements. Dream boards, where you cut out pictures of your desires and paste them to poster boards or bulletin boards, have been used for years and have worked miracles in the lives of millions.

THE PROCESS OF THE "I AM"

Step 1: Learn what your old limiting beliefs are and recognize how you are feeding them.

Your subconscious mind is storing the limiting belief, and your conscious mind is feeding it by your daily thoughts about *lack of, can't do, I'm a victim* thinking. It is also fed by simple negative words we use. As an example, your subconscious mind may be storing an old limiting belief that says, "I will never be free of financial hardship." Your conscious mind will feed that with thoughts like you never got the breaks you needed or it takes money to make money or it's not meant to be. As a result of those thoughts, you are using language like "I can't afford that," or "I will never make that kind of money," or "why does everyone else seem to get all the breaks?" The key is to recognize this and create strong language in a new set of "I am" statements that will switch your mindset back to where it was meant to be.

Step 2: Create new "I am" statements with positive, precise, and powerful language so your subconscious mind feels them.

I have found that short and precise "I am" statements with feeling words are the most powerful.

"I am financially independent and free" versus
"I need more money." The first statement implies
financial abundance and the second implies lack.

When I first wrote the above statement, it said, "*I am financially independent and debt free.*" I used that statement for about a year. I was sharing that statement in a seminar, and an attendee suggested that I take the word "debt" out since it was a negative word. I changed it to "*I am financially independent and free.*" That one word made a huge impact on the effectiveness of the statement.

"*I am toned, strong, and in great shape*" versus "*I am losing weight.*" The first statement implies all the positives of already being in great shape, and the second implies that you need to lose weight, which means you must be overweight.

"*I am an exceptional mother*" versus "*I am a good mom.*" The first statement creates more emotion or feeling. The second implies being good, which is OK, but why not be exceptional?

"*I am enjoying the freedom I feel on my new custom Harley*" versus "*I have a new custom Harley.*" The first statement implies the sensation of cruising down the road on the Harley. You *feel* it. The second is a decent statement but does not convey as much emotion as it could.

"*We are building memories in our new dream home*" versus "*We have a new dream home.*" The first message generates far more feeling than the second one.

We spend lots of time in our seminars coaching people on the language they use in their "I am" statements. It's amazing the difference that one or two key words can make in an "I am" statement.

Step 3: State the "why" behind each statement or desire. You must have a compelling enough "why" to accomplish your desires.

Over the course of nineteen years we faced hundreds of setbacks on our journey to creating a system to help people act on promptings. We had numerous people tell us, over and over, that what we wanted to do could not be done. We faced financial hardships and were presented with other opportunities that would have, at the time, been more comfortable for us. But one thing stood out: I made a promise to my brother that I would act on my promptings and help others do the same. That became my "why," and it was big enough to get past all the "hows."

You will notice the "why" statements in my dream card examples used as many of the senses as possible. When explaining the dream home, I talked about how it looked, how it smelled, how the wood floors sounded when you walked across them, and how relaxing the rooms were. I then visualized it all with pictures on the dream card. The more senses you use in your "why" statement, the more emotion or feeling you generate.

Step 4: Visualize your "I am" statements or desires in your life.

Even though this is one of the senses mentioned already, it needs to be its own step in this process—that is how important visualization is. I have been amazed at how visualization has manifested things into reality in my life. I have often said, "If you want to know what someone will own and where they will be in five years, look at the magazines they keep in their home." As an example, I love four-wheelers and snowmobiles. For twenty years I have subscribed to *Dirt Wheels* and *Sno West* snowmobile magazines. Is it any wonder that I have a thirty-foot enclosed toy trailer that carries six four-wheelers in the summer and five snowmobiles in the winter? If you want a new boat, a dream home, a mountain cabin, a strong portfolio, a successful in-home business, or a charity to support, simply subscribe to the magazines that cover those things. There are magazines out there for almost anything.

WHAT'S EASY TO DO IS ALSO EASY NOT TO DO

You have been reading about the "I am" process. It is easy to do. Many people will say, "Well, if it is so easy to do, then how come so many people are not successful?" The answer is simple. Many people are not successful because the "I am" process is also easy not to do.

I have heard many people joke and even laugh about doing the "I am" process. Many of those same people also wonder how I accomplish so much in my life. It's like they don't see the connection. *Hello!* Laugh and doubt all you want, but you cannot argue with results. I attribute every success in my life to the "I am" process. It is that powerful.

THE "I AM" PROCESS IN ACTION

I love to tell the story about my son Bo. He loves to skateboard, and spends hours and hours skating in the back yard and at local skate parks whenever he can get there. When Bo was thirteen years old, he was trying to land a new trick called a "kick flip." This is a difficult trick where he approaches an obstacle and jumps over it. When he gets in the air, he kicks his board so it flips over in the air, lands face up on the ground, and he lands back on the board. This is a cool trick if you can land it.

Bo had been trying to land this trick for several days. He must have tried at least 500 times. I was out watching him and finally made a simple suggestion. I said to Bo, "When you start your approach, say over and over again in your mind, 'I am landing the kick flip; I am landing the kick flip.'" Like a typical thirteen year old, he thought his dad was crazy. He finally agreed to give it a try. On his third attempt he landed the trick perfectly. He went crazy, I went crazy, and Bo became a believer that everything happens first in your mind.

Since this experience Bo has used this technique on several tricks he has been trying to master. Many times Bo has walked in from the backyard to say that he has landed another trick. He has learned how to train his mind to act as if he can already land a difficult trick.

We have all heard the phrase "mind over matter" thousands of times. Do we truly know what it means and what it can do for us? Everything happens in our subconscious mind first. Whatever the subconscious mind is saying, we end up getting in the way of results in our life. Unfortunately, due to being exposed to so much negativity, our subconscious mind has been programmed to be negative. Our results, therefore, are negative.

When Bo was approaching the kick flip, his subconscious mind was naturally saying he would not land the trick. The result was 500 attempts without landing the trick. Notice how simple it was for him to re-program his subconscious mind. By simply stating, "I am landing the kick flip," his conscious mind responded and on the third attempt he landed the trick.

During her high school years my daughter Whitney was on her high school drill team. At a regional competition her team asked if I would come and give them a pep talk at a dinner party the night before the competition.

In a short twenty minutes I taught them some basic principles about the "I am" process. I asked them what they wanted to accomplish as a team. They said they wanted to win their competition. I asked them if there was any team in the state that had better dancers than them. They said no. I asked them why they had never placed better than fifth at a competition. They did not know why.

I then explained to them that the only difference between them and the teams that placed higher than them was what they were thinking and feeling. The better teams in the state expect to win. They believe they are the best. They tell themselves this prior to competing and while they are competing. It helps them to perform at their highest level.

I asked them if they wanted to prepare their minds to win. They said they did. At this point it was simple. I gave each girl an index card and had her write the following: "We are the best team in the state."

I instructed them to repeat the phrase in their minds as many times as possible between that evening and the next morning when they were scheduled to compete. I also instructed them to chant this as a team prior to going out on the floor to compete. They agreed to try it.

The next day they showed up excited to compete. Some of the girls forgot their index cards, so one of the parents went to the store and got new ones. They wrote the message again so every girl had the card. Each girl repeated out loud, "We are the best team in the state," and then the team said it together. I happened to walk out the door of the gymnasium as they were lining up for their first performance. Their coach was lined up in front of the team. I walked up to her and said,

"Hey, did you know that this team right here is the best team in the state?" The girls went crazy.

So what happened?

As mentioned, to that point this team had never finished better than fifth in a competition. On this day they finished with two first places, two second places, and a third place. They scored a second place overall in the competition. The girls were excited out of their heads. It was an experience I will not soon forget. It is an experience a bunch of seventeen year old girls will remember for a lifetime.

Keep in mind they had only learned about this technique twelve hours prior to competing. They were not sure if it would work and they did not have much time to do it. The improvement on their performance was astounding.

This shows all of us the power of sending the right thoughts and messages to ourselves. Remember, you deserve exactly what you send out. Your mind will work miracles for you if you use it the right way. We all want to make a difference in the world. We all want to reach out and nurture relationships. We all want to acquire wealth in our lives. We all have competitions we want to win, goals we want to reach, and dreams we want to come true.

It's like Walt Disney said: "When you wish upon a star, makes no difference who you are. Anything your heart desires will come to you." I have learned how to wish upon a star. May we all send out our desires to the star we have in our subconscious mind. May we surround those desires with the positive energy that only comes from sending out the positives to ourselves and to others.

"Go to inspirational meetings, get to know men and women who are doing inspiring things. Above all, run as hard as you can from the cynics and gripers and the negativists. They are not going anywhere. You are."

NORMAN VINCENT PEALE

"The secret of achievement is to hold a picture of a successful outcome in mind."

HENRY DAVID THOREAU

CHAPTER 4

The Stories in Your Mind Become the Stories of Your Life

WE ARE CHAMPIONS

When our son Sawyer was fourteen, he played on the ninth-grade football team. They had an amazing season where they had eight wins and two losses on the year. They went all the way to the championship game in their league.

I had the opportunity to work with this team teaching powerful Law of Attraction principles. We taught them that the "stories in their mind become the stories of their lives." I taught them to create the right stories in their mind with "I am" statements. We had them learn the statements of their teammates, and they would yell their teammates' statements out when we threw them the ball. The team had its own "I am" statement: "We are champions." On the playing field the team captains would yell out, "We are," and the team would say, "Champions." They would then hit their thigh pads three times with their hands. When they did this they were inspired, and we were inspired as we watched. The story in their mind became "we are champions."

To put that statement into action, the team followed their coach and worked hard on the fundamentals of the game. They learned their plays and practiced executing them.

They went out on the field as champions. They played as champions. They won eight games as champions. In their minds they were champions, and that is how they played.

They made it to the championship game, and went up against their crosstown rivals. This was an undefeated team with players much bigger than ours. This team beat their opponents by an average of thirty-five points per game. This was a true David versus Goliath kind of story. Our team went into the championship game and played hard against this team. The game was scoreless until close to the end of the first half when their rival team scored a touchdown and went into halftime with a 7-0 lead. Our team went into halftime like champions. Some were discouraged, but overall they still believed they were champions and would win this game. They made their second half game plan and marched proudly onto that field. With heads held high they fought another grueling battle. Early in the second half, their opponent scored another touchdown and went up 14-0. With their backs against the wall they kept on fighting. They made some great plays, exciting runs and catches, and impressive defensive plays. As a proud parent my voice was gone from yelling and screaming with excitement.

This is when you would expect the story to turn and we would tell you about a great comeback that led to victory. After all, isn't that how all the stories end in the movies? Well, it did not quite work out that way. With two minutes left in the game we were still down 14-0. The other team had the ball. I began to wonder how our team would take this defeat. After all, the story in their mind was that they were champions. They believed they were champions, yet they were about to lose the championship game. As the seconds ticked away the reality set in that we had lost the game. Our team went out and shook hands and congratulated the other team. They looked on in silence as the other team celebrated. They walked off the field and gathered together for the coaches meeting. Their fans cheered for them as they knelt down in their traditional post game circle. Parents and friends gathered around that team and its coaches. Each of the coaches talked about the great season they had and how proud they were of the players.

I had a prompting the coach would ask me to say something to the team; sure enough, he did. With emotions running high I walked into the middle of these players, and this is what I said: "Every one of you learned some valuable lessons this year about life. You learned that the stories in your mind become the stories of your life and that you have control over the stories you put in your mind."

When I finished this statement, I yelled out, "Is that right?"

Together the team yelled back, "Yes, sir!"

I went on, "You learned this year what it means to be a champion." Then I yelled out, "Is that right?"

Together the team yelled back, "Yes, sir!"

I went on, "Don't you *ever, ever, ever* stop believing in who you are. Have you got that?"

Together the team yelled back, "Yes, sir!"

I then yelled the words, "WE ARE," and they yelled "CHAMPI-ONS!" I said, "WE ARE," and they yelled "CHAMPIONS!" I said, "WE ARE," and they yelled "CHAMPIONS!"

The story in their mind truly became the story of their life. They went home as champions.

How many of us go home as champions even though we may not have won a battle or accomplished a goal? How many of us stop believing in our positive stories just because we experience setbacks or things don't happen as quickly as we would like?

If you want your "I am" statements or affirmations to work for you in life, you must always believe in them. Too often we find that a setback or a disappointment changes the story in our mind, changes our statements about ourselves, and changes the language we use and the messages we send out to our subconscious mind.

Winners are always winners in their own minds. Champions are always champions in their own minds. The boys on this football team will go on to play more games. There are many seasons left in them. They will go forward as champions in their minds.

The day will come when they take the trophy home. It might be on next year's football team. It might be twenty years from now when they walk across a stage and accept a big award. It might be a quiet moment in meditation when they realize their life is complete and they are at peace. The trophies that you take home will be presented in many different ways so long as you always believe that you are a champion.

"We are"
Champions!

"We are"
Champions!

"We are"
Champions!

Don't you *ever, ever, ever* stop believing in who you are. *You are a champion!*

THESE ARE MY STORIES

When I was young, my mother always told me I had an ear for music. This created a story in my mind that I was good with music. I used to play the piano, and I enjoyed making up my own music. I also loved to write. I would write little short stories, poems, and inspirational thoughts. I told myself I was a great writer. This created a story in my mind that I would make a difference as a writer.

Somewhere along the line I got this idea that I could put both of these gifts together. Why not write songs? With that in my mind I created a desire to write songs, but I never did until later in life. Even though I lived for close to thirty years without ever writing a song, the story of being a songwriter was still in my mind. When I started writing "I am" statements and teaching "I am" principles, I wrote a statement that said, "I am an exceptional songwriter." After all, if I was going to write songs, I might as well write them exceptionally. So I wrote this statement down and started reading it often.

About a year went by, and I hadn't done any songwriting. I went to Las Vegas and met with my convention production crew as we were planning for an upcoming event. We went to a music studio where I met a guy by the name of Sean Galloway. He is a music producer who has a studio built into his garage. This man is amazingly talented. His ability to produce any kind of music we need is incredible.

The first time I met Sean, I was inspired by his talent and the music it produced. We worked on some pieces for our convention intro and for segments throughout the upcoming two-day event. While we were there, I asked Sean to create a series of music tracks I could buy the copyrights to. He produced ten tracks of music and loaded them on my iPod. About a month later I was traveling on an airplane and got out my iPod to listen to some music. As I was scrolling through the selections I came upon the ten tracks produced by Sean and began to listen. I will never forget as I started listening to track seven. The music was beautiful. It resonated with me at that moment. I listened to track seven a few times and was inspired to pull out my journal. I began to write the lyrics to the first song I would ever write. I wrote words that would flow with the music I was listening to at that time.

It took me a total of thirty minutes to write the entire song. You see, I had written an "I am" statement two years previously that said, "I am an exceptional songwriter." My subconscious mind had been sent that message a thousand times. It believed the message, and I wrote the song.

In the previous months I had been speaking a lot about "I am" statements and how those statements become our stories. In our seminars I was teaching that the stories we create in our mind become the stories of our life. This concept was on my mind, and the song I wrote became known as "Stories." I would like to share with you the lyrics of this song:

"STORIES"

These are my stories, the chances of life, they run through my head, and I just gotta be bold, and I gotta be strong. These are my dreams, they're bigger than life, I never let up, I gotta reach for my goals, and I gotta move on.

I get up in the morning, I get up out of bed, I've got these stories running through my head.
It started young, collected two or three, stories of my life only I could see.
Imagination had full control, it's up to me; it's my destiny.
I get to choose the stories on my mind, good or bad only I can find.

*They're never real when they begin, it's up to me if I lose
or win, some are good and some are bad, imagination
makes us happy or sad.
They're never real when they begin, it's up to me if I lose
or win, some are good and some are bad, imagination
makes us happy or sad.*

*These are my stories, the chances of life, they run through
my head, and I just gotta be bold, and I gotta be strong.
These are my dreams, they're bigger than life, I never let
up, I gotta reach for my goals, and I gotta move on.*

*I get up in the morning, and I follow my fate.
Settle for good, or will I make it great?
You've heard it said, perception is real.
Experience is how I feel.
Stories in my mind, stories in my world, one affects the
other, and my life's unfurled.
Some are reality, some are dreams.
When they come together, do I cry or do I sing?*

*They're never real when they begin, it's up to me if I lose
or win.
Some are good and some are bad, imagination makes
you happy or sad.
They're never real when they begin, it's up to me if I lose
or win.
Some are good and some are bad, imagination makes
you happy or sad.*

These are my stories, the chances of life, they run through my head, and I just gotta be bold, and I gotta be strong. These are my dreams, they're bigger than life, I never let up, I gotta reach for my goals, and I gotta move on.

These are my dreams, I gotta believe, I gotta achieve, and I just gotta be strong. And I just gotta be strong.

I took those lyrics back to Sean's music studio in Las Vegas. He introduced me to a young and talented singer named Rushan Reed. The three of us sat in that studio as Rushan sang through the lyrics and Sean adjusted the music tracks to create the final version. This was an incredible experience. When we completed the song, we knew we had something special. We brought my show producer Joe Kenemore in to take it one step further. We created a music video to go along with the song.

We really do control the stories of our life. They really do begin with our imagination, and we have full control of them.

That which happens in our mind becomes our reality down the road. It's like creating a blueprint before you build a building. Everything starts with the blueprint, and construction does not even begin until the blueprint is completed and studied.

The story we create in our mind is the blueprint for what we build in our life. It happens that way every single time. Unfortunately, many people create bad stories in their minds. They end up with a bad blueprint for building their future, and you see it in their decisions and in their results. Fortunately, we have control of this. As the song says, "We get to choose the stories in our mind, good or bad only we can find." When we choose good stories in our minds, it creates a positive blueprint for building our future.

Let's continue to learn from the lyrics of the "Stories" song.

"They're never real when they begin; it's up to me if I lose or win."

What is it that's never real when they begin? The stories in our mind. We make them up—the bad ones and the good ones. If we feed ourselves the bad ones, we lose. But if we nourish ourselves with the good ones, we win. The key to making this work for you is to create a lot more good stories in your mind than bad ones. The "I am" process dramatically helps you create the good stories. That is why those who have mastered the "I am" process are winners.

"Some are good and some are bad; imagination makes us happy or sad."

As we already mentioned some stories are good and some are bad, and both kinds begin with your imagination. Good ones make you happy, and bad ones make you sad. The great news here is that we have complete control of our imagination—that is, if we consciously exercise our imagination to create the stories we desire. If we don't exercise our imagination, it gets lazy and out of shape. It's the lazy imagination that picks up the negative around it and entertains the wrong kind of stories.

How do you exercise your imagination? Simply think great thoughts, dream big dreams, and expose yourself to good stuff every day, like great books, inspiring movies, motivational music, and things that simply make you feel good.

"I get up in the morning, and I follow my fate; settle for good or will I make it great?"

This line is a subtle play on words. It introduces a philosophy about fate. You see, I believe that those who believe in fate will always settle. Those who believe in destiny will always make things great. So if you are getting up in the morning and following your fate, you will be settling, hopefully for good, but settling nonetheless.

To make things great, you need to create your destiny, take control of your life, and choose the stories in your mind. Make them great stories and believe in them.

"You've heard it said, perception is real. Experience is how I feel."

Perception is a thought, even a belief of something we become aware of through the senses. By seeing, tasting, smelling, hearing, and feeling things in our life, we create our experience of everything around us. Our perceptions are nourished by our emotions. Have you ever noticed that when you feel good on the inside, everything on the outside has a more positive appearance? In fact, things taste better, you pick up pleasant aromas, you hear beautiful music or conversation, you see beauty all around you, and you feel good. Everything is in harmony; you are in balance; you are in the flow. Why? Something made you feel good. That feeling or emotion created your perception of the reality around you. It is very real. It becomes your experience, and every experience begins with how you feel.

You can create positive or negative perception depending on how you nourish your thoughts. Studies have shown that 87 percent of everything you are exposed to is negative. When you allow negativity in, you digest that negativity into your thoughts. What you pick up through your senses becomes negative—you do not feel good, you are out of balance, and as a result your emotions run out of control. You then perceive things in a negative way, and that becomes your experience.

A simple way to illustrate this is with the two-phase Road Rage Challenge. This is how it works:

PHASE #1

Get in your car, turn on the radio, and tune into a popular talk show or news station and drive. When another driver cuts you off or drives slowly in front of you, recognize what happens with your emotions. You immediately get upset.

Why?

You are likely listening to news or commentary on the radio that makes you feel bad. Because you feel bad, you begin to notice bad, and you notice it with many of your senses. When the inevitable traffic incident happens, the spark ignites. Your perception is created, and it becomes your reality.

These little daily incidents literally ruin the days of millions of drivers around the world. They go home holding on to the negative emotion, and it carries to other areas of their lives. Seems silly, doesn't it?

PHASE #2

This is where it gets fun. This time, before you begin to drive, think of someone you want to express appreciation to. A simple *thank you, I'm thinking of you*, or even a needed apology. Purchase a greeting card or, even better, use SendOutCards.com online and express your appreciation in writing to the person that came to mind.

Do this right before you drive somewhere. Send the card and then start driving. When another driver cuts you off or drives slowly in front of you, recognize what happens. Chances are you won't even notice.

Why?

You are likely experiencing the "feel-good" emotion created by sending someone a card. You are in a completely different state of mind. This time you feel good, and you begin to notice the good around you with many of your senses. Your perception is created, and it becomes your reality.

I am actually in the habit of starting every day by sending a heart-felt greeting card to someone that comes to mind. This simple activity puts me in an instant state of "feel good." It creates positive and balanced emotion. My perception of the world around me is positive. I experience a high level of energy, and it allows me to experience the world the way it was meant to be experienced. Experience, indeed, is how you feel.

"Stories in my mind, stories in my world, one affects the other, and my life is unfurled. Some are reality, some are dreams, when they come together, do I cry or do I sing?"

These lyrics describe a cycle we all experience. The stories in your mind become the stories in your world or your reality. Your reality affects the stories you continue to create in your mind. I'm sure you have heard the saying, "The rich get richer and the poor get poorer." Why do you think that is? The story in your mind (imagination) creates the story in your world (reality). The story in your world (reality) feeds new stories in your mind (imagination). People who experience financial abundance have created a story of abundance, and they have created abundance that feeds new stories of abundance. The cycle is working the right way for those people. People who struggle financially work with the exact same cycle—it's just heading in the opposite direction.

The same cycle applies to all areas of our lives—finances, relationships, health, and well-being. One story affects the other, and your life is unfurled. As we mentioned some of these stories are reality, and some are dreams. When they come together, do I cry or do I sing?

There comes that time when the story in your mind crosses that threshold and becomes real. So when your stories cross the threshold, or when they come together, do you cry in sadness or do you sing with joy? The choice is yours.

What are the cynics saying right now?

The cynics read this stuff or hear it and what do they think? Unfortunately, those who are in a negative mindset do not see or believe in a connection between what is real and what is imagined. They have been led, by their experiences, to think that reality is all there is and a person has very little control of it.

What a sad way to think. The cynics' beliefs are fed by fear and guilt. They worry their way into cynical thinking.

Susan Jeffers, author of *Feel the Fear and Do it Anyway*, describes the cynic as someone who might believe positive thinking is fine but does not reflect reality. The accusation is that it's too "Pollyanna." But Jeffers asks, "If 90 percent of what we worry about never happens (as studies demonstrate), how is negativity more 'realistic' than positivity?" She goes on to say, "The fact is that what is realistic is up to us, depending on how we shape our thoughts."

Cynics are caught in the conscious mind where rational and realistic thinking are the norm. They like it here because they feel safe. Most people rest here, so they have lots of company. They are not considered different or unrealistic. They feel part of a large group of

PROMPTINGS: YOUR INNER GUIDE TO MAKING A DIFFERENCE

"normal thinkers." The challenge to this is that the conscious mind is where normal happens. The subconscious mind is where exceptional happens. It's where uniqueness is created, and it's where destinies are fulfilled.

In *Power of the Subconscious Mind,* Joseph Murphy suggests that "the subconscious is an entirely different kettle of fish to the conscious mind. It cannot be coerced, responding best to relaxed faith that it will do its transforming work with ease. Along with relaxed faith, the ease with which the subconscious accomplishes things increases with emotion."

Listen to the words being used here: ease, emotion, relaxed faith. These words are not used much with the rational, conscious thinker. They use words like force and process, and they use fear as the motivator to take action. Because of this, a cynic is created, and human potential is not fully realized.

What are the optimists saying right now?

The optimists reading this book are probably reading the lyrics to the stories song over again, and they are being inspired by it. Why? Because they believe the message. It resonates with them, gives them hope, and helps them focus on possibility.

The optimists' beliefs are nourished with *faith* and *love.* They excite themselves into positive thinking. The optimist is flourishing in the subconscious mind, where imagination and feelings are the norm. This is where possibilities are explored and greatness manifests into reality.

Murphy goes on to say that "an idea or a thought alone may excite the rational, conscious mind, but the subconscious likes things to be emotionalized. When a thought becomes a feeling, and imagination becomes desire, it will deliver what you want with speed and abundance."

THE STORY IN YOUR MIND

The stories in your mind are the workings of your subconscious. They do become the stories of your life where your conscious mind dwells. If you allow the workings of your subconscious to fulfill its potential, then your conscious world becomes a pleasant and positive experience.

The famous psychologist William James observed, "Whatever people expect to be true will be so." The subconscious is where your imagination has full control and you can create whatever expectation you like. For all you conscious thinkers, there is a process. The story in your mind should always come first and be created with the faith that the subconscious allows. The story of your life should always follow. If you allow the process to work in this order, you will see your own unique potential fulfilled.

"A positive attitude may not solve all your problems but it will annoy enough people to make it worth the effort."

HERM ALBRIGHT

"There is nothing either good or bad but thinking makes it so."

SHAKESPEARE

CHAPTER 5

Good or Bad Only You Can Find

My dad is a master storyteller. He has been telling stories to everyone around him for more than sixty years. I have often heard him say life is a collection of stories. That statement has had a profound influence in my life. In fact, I believe it to be one of the most powerful tools you can use on your personal-development journey.

Think about it: Life is nothing more than an ongoing collection of stories. If we were to simply focus every day on collecting a good story so we could share it with others, how great would your life be? That is how my dad has lived his life. He is known as the eternal optimist. He finds the good in every situation. He has faced many trials and tribulations in his life, but you would never know it. People ask him how he stays so positive, and I have the answer: My dad is so busy looking for the next cool story to tell he doesn't focus on the negative things that might be happening.

Whether we know it or not, we are collecting stories every day of our lives. We collect stories in our mind with our imaginations, and we collect stories in our world by living each day. The stories we collect in our mind have a dramatic impact on the stories that happen to us in life. As the lyrics of the "Stories" song indicates, "We get to choose the stories in our mind, good or bad only we can find."

If we get to choose the stories in our mind, why would anyone choose, find, or collect bad stories? That doesn't make sense. Part of the reason people choose bad stories in their mind is because they simply do not know they are doing it. If you were to internalize the thought that "Life is a collection of stories" and that you have full control of the stories you create in your mind, then you would begin to collect better stories.

REMEMBER THE LYRICS?

Stories in my mind, stories in my world. One affects the other and my life is unfurled.

The challenge is that people work backwards with this concept. They collect stories in their world first. Those stories dictate the stories they put in their mind. This is not a good idea. If you collect stories in your mind first, where you have control of the story, then you can begin to manifest the stories you desire in your life.

The reason my dad is able to tell great stories is because he collects great stories. It has become a daily habit for him to do so. Every morning my dad will offer a silent prayer (story in his mind) that says, "Heavenly Father, please put me in a place today where I might be of service to someone in need." Why does he do that? It makes him feel good, and it makes for some great stories. Remember, my dad is a story collector.

If you work backwards, the world and its negativity will determine the stories you put in your mind. If the stories in your mind now are negative and out of your control, you manifest more negativity in your life. I hear people say all the time, "Why is this happening to me?" or " I can't seem to get any breaks," or "Why do bad things happen to good people?" or "Why do other people seem to get all the breaks?" I have a simple answer to every one of those questions. The reason those things are happening is staring at you in the mirror. It is you. You have collected stories from your outside world, you have internalized those stories into your mind—your subconscious—and you have believed those stories and lost control. But you can turn it around.

TURNING IT AROUND STARTS WITH UNDERSTANDING UNIVERSAL LAWS

What you send out in life is what you get back. This applies to what you send out to others and what you send to yourself. If you have collected a bad story from the life around you and internalized it, you have sent a bad story to your subconscious. What you send out is what you get back. Your subconscious says, "OK," and begins to manifest. It's that simple. This process is called the Law of Attraction.

THE LAW OF ATTRACTION

The Law of Attraction is a simple universal law that has been around since the beginning of time. Just like gravity, the Law of Attraction works whether you believe in it or not.

We have been taught this principle for centuries, and every major religion endorses it. Most of us have heard about it in various forms, but many have not understood exactly what it means or the incredible power that comes from putting it to work in your life.

The things you send out to yourself and to others are sent through thoughts, feelings, words, and deeds. If you send out positive, you get back positive. If you send out negative, you get back negative. It sounds so simple, but here is the challenge. As much as 90 percent of our exposure from the world is negative. This means the Law of Attraction will often be working in a negative way in our lives, rather than a positive way.

As an example, by the time a child reaches four years of age they have been told "you can't do that" or "you don't want that" over 16,000 times, and 80,000 times by age ten. She is already associating things she wants with "bad" or "negative." Another study showed that 95 percent of our children enter public schools with a high self-esteem. Only 5 percent leave public schools with a high self-esteem. Why is this? I believe it has to do with the fact that we are born to dream but are taught that dreams are bad.

Think about it. Children have incredible imaginations. They can and will conquer the world. Anything is possible to them. They naturally send out positive thoughts, feelings, and words to the universe— that is, until they get the 16,000 messages of "you can't," "you won't," and "you should" from all the people around them. They are taught to reprogram their natural thinking to the thinking of the world. As a result they begin to send out the negative. They associate wants with bad, so they begin thinking about *don't wants*, and the Law of Attraction responds. This is why so many people go through life not getting the things they want.

Children dwell in the subconscious with their imaginations. Adults dwell in the conscious with their doubts. We have already established that dwelling in the conscious mind produces normal status-quo living. Dwelling in the subconscious produces greatness. How, then, did we allow ourselves to grow up and move from the subconscious to the conscious? Parents would explain that they have to be realistic. They must teach their children basic principles. After all, if you put your beautiful little hand on the hot stove, you will get hurt. If you run out into the street without looking both ways, you might get run over. If you draw on the walls, it will make a mess. Many parents would say these incidents contribute to the 16,000 messages of "no" and "don't do that" children receive by the age of four.

This is a true statement, and parents do need to teach basic principles. But how can we teach these basics without robbing our children of their imaginations? If we as parents are living in the conscious world, believing the cynical way of thinking, watching the news and doubting, focusing on realism rather than possibility, then we might be crossing the line with our children. You might be teaching those basics, but you also might be taking away from the vibrant imaginations your children dwell in.

Children naturally think of the things they want, and adults unnaturally think of the things they don't want. *Don't want* thinking is unnatural because you have to learn it. *Do want* thinking is natural because you were born doing it. *Don't want* thinking begins with a story collected from the outside world. *Do want* thinking begins with a story created in your mind.

In her book *Excuse Me, Your Life Is Waiting,* Lynn Grabhorn explains, "What we are thinking about and how it makes us feel is what we get back. You can focus on *don't wants* or focus on *do wants*. It's the feelings that create the energy we send out. Reality is nothing more than the result of how we have been flowing our energy."

In other words, *don't want* thinking creates a negative energy flow, and *do want* thinking creates a positive energy flow.

I love her use of words: "flowing our energy." This is exactly what we do. We flow our energy in a negative and destructive way (*don't wants*) or a positive and productive way (*do wants*). And guess what? We choose the stories that create the energy flow. It really is that simple.

If you do not like your current situation in life, simply look at the stories you are sending yourself and notice the direction of your energy flow. It is either moving you away from your desires or moving you toward them, and you are the only person who created the energy flow. Now you can lie to yourself or deny that you have anything to do with where you are. You can certainly blame someone else. After all, that's an easy thing to do and it takes the pressure off yourself. The only problem is those things don't work. As T. Harv Eker says, "You can be rich or you can be a victim, but you can't be both." I have observed, in myself and in others over the years, that we all have blind spots. And our blind spots are blocking us from seeing who created the energy flow in our own lives.

BLIND SPOTS

If you are driving down the road and you look in your side-view mirror, you can see other vehicles coming up behind you. You can see them up to a certain point, and then they disappear. That is why, when you're learning to drive, you are taught to look in your side-view mirror, then look over your left shoulder to check what is called your blind spot. This ensures you are safe to change lanes. How often do close calls, road rages, and even accidents happen because people fail to check their blind spot?

The same thing happens in our lives. How often do we cause friction and even disaster because of the thoughts we have, language we use, or excuses we make—and we can't see them? They are blind spots, and they keep you from where you want to go. They keep you from hearing the inner promptings attempting to guide you to your genius within.

THE STORIES OF NICK AND TARA

Nick was a guy who worked for the railroad. Nick showed up for work one day and learned that everyone would be getting off early to celebrate a birthday for one of his co-workers. Like everyone else Nick was excited to get off early and enjoy the party. It was approaching the early quitting time. Nick entered a railroad car to do his routine maintenance work. He shut the door, and it locked from the outside. Nick began to panic. It just so happened this was a refrigerated boxcar, and Nick knew his co-workers would be leaving soon. He pounded on the door as he yelled and screamed for help. Nobody heard him. Closing time came and went. Everyone left, and Nick was stuck in the refrigerated boxcar.

Nick began to write down his fears. He wrote things like, "I'm afraid I might freeze to death in here. My ears and fingers are getting cold. I don't think I can make it through the night." The next morning, when Nick's co-workers showed up for work, they opened the boxcar and found Nick laying on the floor. Sure enough, he had frozen to death. The problem with this story is that the refrigerator on the boxcar was broken. It never got below 59 degrees Fahrenheit in that car the whole night. Nick literally thought himself to death. He was sending strong messages to his subconscious that he was freezing to death. His subconscious, as it always does, said, "OK," and sent messages to the body that it was freezing. The result? He froze to death at 59 degrees.

❋

Tara grew up believing she was Miss America. Not that she would become Miss America or that someday it might happen—she *was* Miss America. The story in her mind was already established. Her inner prompting told her who she was.

In 1994 she entered the Miss Florida pageant and won the title of first runner-up. She decided to try again; after all, she was not first runner-up—she was Miss America. She entered the Florida pageant again, and once again she won the prize as first runner-up. Tara was tempted to get down and discouraged, but she didn't do that. She stayed focused on her goal. After all, she was not first runner-up—she was Miss America in her own mind.

She decided she needed to change her environment, so she moved to Kansas, and in 1997 she entered the Miss Kansas pageant and won the title. That same year she went on to be crowned Miss America. Tara Holland saw her dream come true.

In an interview after the pageant someone asked Tara the secret to her success. She admitted that after she had lost twice in a row at the state-level competitions, she had been tempted to give up, but instead she went out and rented dozens of videos of local pageants, state pageants, Miss Teen, Miss Universe, Miss World—whatever she could find. She rented hundreds of videos of various pageants and watched them over and over again.

As Tara watched each young woman crowned a winner, she pictured herself in that situation. She pictured herself receiving the crown. She pictured herself walking down the runway in victory. Time and time again she envisioned herself winning. Seeing herself as a winner, Tara said, was the key to her success.

Another reporter asked her if she was nervous walking down the runway in front of millions of people watching on television and with the announcer singing the famous Miss America song.

Tara's response was interesting. "No, I wasn't nervous at all," she said. "You see, I had walked down that runway thousands of times before."

The stories of Nick and Tara illustrate the power of stories we use. Nick's story led him to disaster. Tara's story led her to her genius within. She was nourishing her inner prompting that told her she was not only Miss America, but a woman making a positive impact in the lives of millions of people.

I have had the good fortune of meeting Tara Dawn Christensen. She is an amazing wife, mother, and role model. To this day she delivers powerful speeches and makes a difference everywhere she goes. I have not had the chance to meet Nick because he is *dead*!

THE CHOICE IS YOURS

We get to choose the stories in our mind *good or bad only we can find*. So, why would anyone choose bad stories?

> *They don't know they are doing it*
>
> *They allow stories in their world to create the stories in their minds*
>
> *They have ongoing thoughts that feed those stories*
>
> *They use language in their conversations that feed those stories*
>
> *They have created blind spots they don't see or they deny they created their own bad story*

How then do you consistently choose good stories? (This is not rocket science, folks.)

>*Know that you collect stories every day, so choose to collect good ones*
>
>*Create desired stories in your mind by using your imagination, and allow them to become the stories of your life*
>
>*Entertain ongoing thoughts that nourish your good stories*
>
>*Use language that nourishes your good stories*
>
>*Be willing to check your blind spots and take responsibility*

This is how you turn it around. This is how you begin to truly hear your inner promptings. Those inner promptings are telling you, every day, who you are. They will guide you to your genius and allow you to live the good stories of life.

Lynn Grabhorn says, "You never again have to believe that circumstances outside of you control your life. You never again have to believe it is wrong to want. You never again have to believe that anyone or anything other than you is in control of your life."

I have used this "turn it around" process in my own life, and I have coached many people through the same process. It almost always works. The only time I have ever seen this not work for someone is when they have had an issue with one simple word. I have seen this word create major roadblocks for people. It even gets in the way of someone's ability to control their energy flow or to create positive stories for themselves. I have seen people run and hide from this word.

I have watched this word create negative energy and controversial debate. This one word is *deserve*!

It is amazing to me how many people believe they do not deserve the blessings of life. Some people believe because they have made mistakes (who doesn't?) or did not do enough good in the world, they don't deserve the good stories to happen to them.

I have conducted seminars where I facilitated open discussion on this subject, and it was amazing to hear the conversation this word created. When I find someone in a seminar who does not believe she deserves the best that life has to offer, I will call her by name and say, "Jamie, so what you are saying is that you don't deserve the good things in life that you desire."

She will say, "Yes."

I will then ask who came with her to the seminar. She will point to a good friend or family member next to her. I will ask her to describe that person to the audience. Every time I do this, people go on to describe the amazing person sitting next to them and how much they adore him or her.

When they finish, I will say, "So, Jamie, does your friend Sara deserve the very best that life has to offer?"

Every time she will say, "*Absolutely.*"

I then say, "Why is Sara any different than you?"

This usually creates cheers from the audience and an "aha" moment for the Jamies of my audiences.

There have been times when, after this interaction, the Jamies of the audience still have a challenge with this. If they do, I will ask the friend, "So, Sara, does your friend Jamie deserve the very best that life has to offer?"

She will always say, "*Absolutely.*"

The debating stops after this. People seem to get it. I hope and pray they leave the seminar and get it for the rest of their lives.

❉

Lynn Grabhorn says, "Deserving has nothing to do with how good we are or how smart we are or how hard we work. It only has to do with the energy that we send out."

In other words, you deserve exactly what you send out. Whatever you send out to others through thoughts, feelings, words, or deeds is what you will get back. Whatever you send out to yourself through your thoughts, feelings, words, or deeds is what you will get back.

If you create a good story in your mind, your subconscious gives back a good story in your life. If you create a good story and then think you don't deserve it, then the game is over. You blocked the natural process of manifesting your desires into your world.

You are unique; there are things in this life that only you can do, and you are deserving of everything that you send out to yourself and to others. Don't ever allow anyone to tell you different. Nobody decides your worthiness but you. If you have an issue with deserving, you will have a difficult time finding the good stories of life.

FINAL TIPS ON CONSISTENTLY FINDING GOOD STORIES
Focus on the things you want, not on the things you don't want.

Here is some interesting information on *do wants*: We have been brainwashed into believing that most wants are not only self-serving no-no's, but impossible. As a result you associate *wants* with *bad* or *unreachable*. You need to identify your wants and state them in present tense ("I am" statements). Feel good about your wants. Don't wish for them; yearn for them. *Just feel good about your wants.* This is essential to finding the good stories in your mind and in your life.

Focus on the thoughts you entertain

Studies have shown we process over 50,000 thoughts per day, and the majority of our thoughts, if not monitored, are negative. Be aware of the thoughts you entertain. Your thoughts are often displayed in your self-talk. What kinds of things are you saying to yourself? What are your conversations when you are alone in the shower, in your car, or wherever you process your thoughts?

WHAT DO YOU SAY WHEN YOU TALK TO YOURSELF?

My two sons laugh at their dad because they always catch me talking to myself. One of my favorite places to have self-discussion is in the hot tub. They will sneak up on me so they can laugh, because I'm in there talking out loud to myself.

What am I saying? I am often processing my next speech or seminar. I am rehearsing how a meeting or conversation needs to go the following day. I am taking a relationship in conflict and speaking to that person in a positive way. Laugh if you want, but I like myself. I have great conversations with myself. This is my opportunity to process my thoughts in a positive way. Self-talk is a way to process those 50,000 thoughts and turn them into something positive.

Because I focus on *do wants* and create desired stories in my mind, I naturally have great thoughts to process. I'm not watching the news, listening to talk shows, entertaining the latest gossip, or trying to find what's wrong with the world. Trust me, the people who are close to me won't allow it. Anytime I slip up and say anything negative, my family and close friends never let me hear the end of it. This is good because it reminds me that I have no room to entertain "stinkin' thinkin,'" as Zig Ziglar would say.

Focus on the language you use in every conversation

Certain words should be taken out of your vocabulary and carefully replaced. Try to implement the following:

Problem replaced with *challenge*

Can't afford replaced with *choose to spend money differently*

Strange replaced with *interesting*

Hate replaced with *love*

Try replaced with *do*

Can't replaced with *will* or *won't*

Barrier replaced with *possibility*

Need replaced with *have*

This list could go on and on. In fact, I challenge you to add to this list. Every time you find yourself using a word you know is a negative, low-energy word, find a word to replace it and add it to your list. The language we use is amazingly powerful, especially as we create the stories we desire in our minds. The subconscious feels things, so words that create feel-good emotions will help those stories to manifest as stories in our life.

The lyrics of the song say, "Good or bad only you can find." Because of that, throughout this chapter we have made reference to "good stories" and "bad stories." In the use of everyday language I would recommend if you say you are going to create a good story, you might as well enhance that by saying you are creating exceptional stories. That is a single word change, and look at the difference. Exceptional is a whole lot better than good.

"The time is always right to do what is right."

MARTIN LUTHER KING JR.

"Take time to deliberate; but when the time for action arrives, stop thinking and go in."

ANDREW JACKSON

"I must lose myself in action lest I wither in despair."

ARTHUR HALLAM

CHAPTER 6

Balance Between Affirmation and Action

So far we have discussed the inner promptings and the stories we create in our mind. We have focused on self, and we have explored the affirmation process. We have learned that affirmations are most effective as "I am" statements, and *those statements are an extension of our inner promptings.* They represent who we are. The power of the "I am" statement is that you already are what your statement says. Those who learn and believe this are those who manifest success quickly in their life.

Over the years I have been a committed student of personal development. I have read hundreds of books, attended seminars, listened to tapes, and written in journals. I have loved the process and have learned some amazing things. One thing I have noticed is there is great information about self-development and the use of affirmation. There is also great information about processes and action plans—things like time and task management as well as step-by-step "how-to" programs.

I have learned that balance is the key to making personal development work. I have learned there are two elements in life that, when evenly balanced, will bring you the highest level of success:

Balance between affirmation and action
and
Balance between self and others

Successful people find balance between affirmation and action.

Affirmations are the stories you create in your mind, and actions are the fundamentals you practice.

You must experience a balance to progress. There are many people who have the affirmation part worked out, but they don't take action. There are others who take action but have the wrong stories in their subconscious mind, where all things are created. It is only when you are in balance that you see significant and quick progress.

Growing up I loved to play basketball. I played on little league, church league, and school teams. We used to go to practice, and my coaches would always spend the majority of practice time on fundamentals—dribbling, bounce passes, shooting, follow-through, defense, and others. When I first started, I couldn't figure out why we didn't play more games during practice. I soon learned that fundamentals are what make the game. You have to practice the fundamentals over and over so you are prepared for the game.

Same thing applies in life. You must take action. Someone who has balance between affirmation and action will experience a process similar to this:

Affirmation Steps

- Inner promptings tell you who you are
- "I am" statements define your inner promptings and nourish your subconscious
- Visualization techniques enhance the nourishment of your subconscious

- "Why" statements using all the senses enhance the nourishment of your subconscious

Action Steps
- Subconscious, not knowing the difference between what's real and imagined, says, "OK," and sends you a "process of action"
- The "process of action" is implemented with daily fundamentals practiced consistently
- With consistency, you get to where you no longer think about the process—you just do it and allow the process to take place

The action steps are where lots of people get caught. They either don't recognize the "process of action" when it shows up, or they simply don't act on it. Part of the challenge is when the action plan shows up, it's not as if it's all detailed with ribbons and bows on it. You are simply guided to take certain steps, and those steps involve daily fundamentals with consistent practice. Consistency gets you to where you no longer think about it—you just do it. This final step is crucial.

Studies have been done that show a process to creating a habit in your life. It's been found there are four steps to creating a habit. When creating good habits for personal growth, most people get caught between levels three and four.

Level Three is called conscious competence—where you think about what you are doing. You are still forcing the process.

Level Four is called unconscious competence—where you no longer think about it; you just do it. You allow the process to flow daily in your life.

You must get to Level Four with whatever process of action you are doing. It takes consistent practice.

In my seminars I illustrate this by tying my shoes two different ways. I will first tie my shoes the way that most people tie their shoes. The challenge I have with this is that I never learned to tie my shoes the normal way. When I tie them the normal way, the audience clearly sees that I am thinking intently about what I am doing. It's a clumsy process, but I do manage to get the shoe tied.

When I was five years old, my mother taught me to tie my shoes the bunny-ear way. You form two bunny-ear loops and tie them. I show the audience how I tie shoes to this day, and they clearly see that I don't think at all about it: I just tie the shoes. It's quick and easy. I am a Level Four bunny-ear shoe-tier.

Many people are really good at the affirmation steps and fall way short on action. Others are really good on action but fall short on affirmation. Of those who are really good at action, many still have challenges with the final step. In fact, in my business I notice that the fine line between those who experience massive success and those who struggle is drawn right here. Many people simply do not get to Level Four. They do not stay consistent with the fundamentals, and they continue to think about what they are doing.

❖

Here is a story about a friend of mine who created balance between affirmation and action.

Scott Ruseler is a tile-flooring contractor. He installs tile floors in large custom homes in Utah. He makes about $60,000 per year. Because he worked around large custom homes every day, he began to visualize himself and his family in a large custom home. He created an "I am" statement in his mind that said, "We are living in our new custom home." He was around these homes every day, so he had a daily visualization of the home of their desires.

Now let me pose a question. How does a guy making $60,000 per year move into a $650,000 home? Simple: He has an "I am" statement in his mind. He creates the feel-good of that statement by visualizing this home every day. Now he simply waits for the "process of action" to show up. Here is what happened: He started doing what other contractors were doing. He built a smaller home and sold it at a profit. He took his profits and financed another home project. Built again, sold again, and made more profit. He got to the point where he no longer thought about the process; he just did it. He was doing this as a side business to his regular income.

In the period of fourteen short months he had amassed enough money to use as collateral on a large construction loan. He was granted that loan. He teamed up with a buddy who had a general contracting license, and he contracted the building of his own dream home. Total construction loan was $375,000. He built the home and used $200,000 of his money and a $175,000 mortgage to pay off the construction loan. When he moved into the home, it appraised for $650,000.

Scott recognized the "process of action" when it showed up. He implemented a daily practice of this process. He did this consistently enough to where he no longer thought about it; he just did it. The result: A $60,000 annual-income earner in a $650,000 dream home.

This friend had some skills and tools that allowed him to build his wealth this way. He practiced daily fundamentals of the construction and real-estate sales process. What he did not know, he learned. Because he created the story in his mind and visualized it, he was able to work every day towards his goal. The two biggest factors that helped him manifest his dream home were that he visualized every day by working in large custom homes, and he was so consistent with his side business that he no longer thought about how he was doing it; he was just doing it.

This reminds me of a family trip we took to Lake Powell in southern Utah. We were there with my family and two other families. In the group we had my two sons Bo and Sawyer and three other teenage boys. We found a place to go cliff jumping. It was a spot that gradually sloped upward so you could jump at different heights. The five teenage boys were up on the cliff showing off for the girls in the boat. They were daring each other to jump off the cliff to the water below. I casually walked up to where they were, walked right between them, and jumped. Little did they know I grew up cliff jumping at Lake Powell, so I had some experience with it. One thing I knew is that once you checked out where you were landing and you knew things were clear, the best way to jump was to not think too much about it—just step off the edge.

After I went off, of course, a few of the boys went off. Bo decided he wanted to walk down a little lower. He got down to where it was about a twenty-foot jump. That is still pretty high and can be intimidating. Bo was on the edge, thinking a whole lot about jumping. I climbed up to where he was and again stepped off the edge without thinking too much about it. After several minutes Bo stood up and, without hesitation, stepped off the edge and safely hit the water below. He swam over to the boat, jumped in, and said, "Dad, it's a lot easier when you don't think about it."

NEW YEAR'S RESOLUTIONS

The challenge people have with New Year's resolutions is they are simply out of balance between affirmation and action.

It was Monday morning, January 2, 2006. As I do every morning, I drove to the health club where I work out. I arrived at 8:30 a.m., drove into the parking lot, and could not find a parking spot anywhere. For the first time in five years of attending this gym the parking lot was completely full. I ended up driving to another parking lot next to the health club property. When I got out of my truck, the manager and part-owner of the club pulled up next to me. I jokingly said, "Wow, the owner of the club can't even park in front of her own place." She laughed and said, "Don't worry, that will all change in about two weeks. This is our annual New Year's resolution crowd."

What she said was funny but sad at the same time. Why is it that people only keep their resolutions for a very short period of time? Part of the challenge is that people's minds are programmed with old behaviors, limiting beliefs, and *don't-want* thinking. In other words, a person thinks, *I am tired of being overweight* or *I don't want to look this way anymore. The solution is to make a New Year's resolution that focuses on going to the gym because I am tired of being overweight.*

What the subconscious mind hears is *I am overweight*. With that, the person goes to the gym for a week or two, finds out that it's not easy to get up early every morning, and then feels frustrated because they are short of breath on the treadmill. Their subconscious mind is sending back to them that they are overweight, so what's the use? It feels better to wake up and have a doughnut with chocolate milk. By the end of the two weeks they have fallen back into the old behavior pattern. The result is this: On January 12 I can drive into the health club parking lot and easily find a place to park.

So the question is, why do I keep driving to the gym? My New Year's resolutions are made and reviewed all year long. I state them in the present tense, as if they already exist. I have index cards listing my goals, which all begin with the words "I am." My health statement says, "I am toned, strong, and in great shape." I set this goal several years ago, and at the time I had thirty pounds to lose. After setting this goal I started going to the gym, and my subconscious mind acted as if I were toned, strong, and in great shape. This kept me going to the gym long enough to create a good habit of working out every morning. Now going to the gym is like brushing my teeth. It is something I have to do every morning. I am at Level Four with going to the gym—I no longer think about it; I just do it.

The key to success with resolutions is to define and flush out bad habits and replace them with good habits. The perfect example was mentioned above. The bad habit was chocolate milk and doughnuts to start the day. It was replaced with the good habit of fifty laps in the pool to start the day.

Along the way, I found some interesting information about New Year's resolutions. **Of those who make resolutions:**

1. Less than 10 percent actually keep them. The most common mistakes are:
    *   Failing to write them down
    *   Making them out of fear of unwanted things or consequences
    *   Failing to believe in them in the first place
2. Of those who do write them down, 63 percent are still keeping them after two months.
3. People make more resolutions to start a new habit than to break an old one.

The top four resolutions made:
1. Increase exercise
2. Be more conscientious about work or school
3. Develop better eating habits
4. Stop smoking, drinking, or using drugs or caffeine

With a proper balance between affirmation and action we are prepared to set goals and make resolutions the right way.

Remember, your subconscious mind does not know the difference between what is real and what is imagined. If you state your goals or make your resolutions in the present tense and you write them down, your mind will kick in and act as if those things are real. Sooner than you think, they become real. Why? Because we know about keeping a balance between affirmation and action. We watch for the process of action to show up, and we begin to consistently practice the fundamentals.

My health statement says, "I am toned, strong, and in great shape." My subconscious says, "OK." The daily fundamentals are things like looking at labels before I purchase food items, working out at the pool, doing push-ups and fast-pace walking, and more. I no longer think about those things; I just do them.

Here is a challenge to be aware of. I got really good at this routine. Then I started traveling more and more with my business. This made the routine more difficult. This is what I found myself saying, thinking, and doing: "Everyone knows you don't eat very well when you are on the road. I can't work out as much because I am in different places." Without even realizing it, I changed my health "I am" statement to something negative. What happened? Ten unwanted pounds came back on, and I knew better. Be careful with the language you allow to creep in. If the story in your mind changes, your actions change.

"We make a living by what we get but we make a life by what we give."

WINSTON CHURCHILL

"I now perceive one immense omission in my psychology. The deepest principle of human nature is the craving to be appreciated."

WILLIAM JAMES

CHAPTER 7

Balance Between Self and Others

My father and I had the opportunity to take a boys' youth group to Lake Powell in southern Utah. This was your typical youth outing at the lake. We were there for three days, and we all had lots of fun together. We did the usual boating kinds of activities—lots of water skiing, tubing, cliff diving, and talking by the fireside at night. The favorite activity was waterskiing, and all the boys participated. One of the boys was the superstar of the group. He was very athletic and the most popular. Another one of the boys was at the opposite end of the spectrum. He was a little slow, physically challenged, and struggled to connect with the other boys.

When the superstar kid skied, everyone paid attention. He would fly across the wake and shoot huge rooster tails of water as he cut back and forth. Everyone made a big deal over how great this kid skied. When the challenged boy tried to ski, it was a totally different story. He would get in the water, put two skis on, and proceed to attempt getting up. Time after time, he would try to get up on those skis. Time after time, he failed. This went on for three days. It finally got to the point where the other boys started to make fun of him.

On the final day a miracle took place. The challenged boy, once again, was trying to get up on the skis. After several attempts the superstar boy stood up in the boat and said he had seen enough of this. He put on his life jacket, jumped into the lake, swam back to the boy, put on the skis, and placed the boy in front of him on the same skis. He told my dad to hit it. As the boat pulled them forward the two boys stood up on the skis and proceeded to ski all the way around the cove of that lake. You should have seen the smile on the face of that challenged young man. This was one of those perfect moments—a memory etched into my mind that has defined what I aspire to be: Someone who will jump in the lake, swim out to another person in need, put on the skis, and help them get up.

We all have this opportunity in our lives. In fact, it is what life is really all about. The challenged boy in this story had physical and mental limitations blocking him from getting up on the skis. There are millions of people around us who are blocked by negative thinking, lack of hope, unseen purpose, feelings of defeat, or feelings of being underappreciated and even unloved. You might be one of them. There are times in our lives when we are the ones who cannot get up on the skis and we need help. There are other times when we have the opportunity to jump in the lake and do the helping. Are we prepared when those times come? Are we willing to accept help when we are the one in need?

Here is the interesting part of this story. After the two boys finished skiing together the challenged boy wanted to attempt getting up one more time on his own. What do you suppose happened? You guessed it. After being shown how by another person who cared, he got up on his own on his first attempt. Often, a simple act of caring is all someone needs to get up on their own. There is an amazing energy around serving and being served. It is the very energy that gives us the stories that make life beautiful.

❖

So far in this book, we have gone into great detail about self-development. We have discussed how to create desired stories in our mind and then manifest them as stories in our life. We have shared the concept that we all have inner promptings telling us who we are. We also enjoy outer promptings that tell us what to do with who we are.

The key to sustaining balance between self and others is to act on both kinds of promptings every day. Know who you are, nourish who you are, develop and improve on who you are, and then *give yourself away*. What good is all your self-development if it doesn't serve someone? Let's go back to the waterski story. The boy who reached out and helped had developed himself. He lifted weights, practiced on the waterskis, played numerous sports, and believed in himself. He enjoyed a quality of life as a result of developing himself. He was the center of attention, and he had a riot out there waterskiing, but what do you suppose was his greatest memory of the trip? To put things into perspective, that trip happened about twenty-five years prior to this writing. Both of those boys are grown men now with families and jobs and goals and dreams. The boy who jumped in to help was acting on an outer prompting. In a brief instant he saw and opportunity to give himself away. He is now spending a lifetime enjoying the memory.

I LOVE YA, MAN!

I had the opportunity to attend a church-owned junior college in southeast Idaho. I was a young twenty-one-year-old student learning who I was and what directions I would take in my life. We had some great times during those college days. We had a church group with about 150 students in it. We attended church together, had weekly activities together, and helped each other with school studies.

At one of the very first activities we had as a group, we were gathered together playing games and getting acquainted. When it was time to leave I stood up and said, "See y'all. *I love ya, man!*" To be perfectly honest, I had no idea where that comment came from. I just blurted it out. Several of the other students looked at me kind of funny and then, hesitantly, said, "Yeah, we love you too."

It was kind of awkward for everyone the first time it was said. It was interesting, though, that after that night, every time someone in our group saw another group member on campus or at our gatherings, you would hear "I love ya, man!" as the parting expression. In fact, it caught on like wildfire, and it bonded our group together in record time. We loved being together. We could not wait to attend the next activity or to run into one of our own on campus.

Soon after this, our group was asked to visit the youth correctional facility for a night of games and activities. As a part of that visit I was asked to close the evening with a motivational message targeted to these troubled teens. I gladly accepted the assignment. I'm not sure why I gladly accepted because I spent the next two weeks racking my brain, trying to figure out what I could say to these kids. I didn't have a clue what I was going to do.

The evening event came. About 100 students from our group took a bus ride out to the correctional facility. When we arrived, the officials had us walk through some doors and down a hallway to a gymnasium. Strangely enough, they had the troubled teens lining both sides of the hallway as we walked between them. Wow! If looks could kill. These kids didn't want us there. It was just another crazy activity the corrections officers had planned for them.

We entered the gym, reluctantly played some games, and had some treats. The time came for me to give my speech. I still had no clue what I was going to say. They gathered the correctional teens and had them sit in the left section of bleachers. Our church group sat in the right section of bleachers. They asked me to come to the front of the group. I slowly walked to the microphone, and just in the nick of time the prompting came. I knew what I was going to do. The challenge was that it involved everyone from my church group, and they did not know what I was going to do. On a leap of faith I plunged forward with my plan.

This is what I did.

Pointing to the left section of bleachers where the corrections group sat, I said, "I want all of you guys to know there is one reason that we came here tonight and on the count of three, our group is going to tell you what it is." Keep in mind, our group had no clue what I was doing. I continued forward yelling out, "One, two, three," and simultaneously 100 students from our church group yelled out the words, "*I love ya, man!*"

I breathed a quick sigh of relief. It actually worked.

"I want to hear it again," I said. "One, two, three."

And again our group yelled out, "*I love ya, man!*"

I said, "I think we need to hear it one more time. One, two, three," and as loud as they could, our group yelled again, "*I love ya, man!*"

I looked those boys in the eyes and softly said, "That is why we came here tonight, because we love ya, man. Thank you for letting us do that."

I was done. Shortest speech I have ever given in my life. As I walked away from the microphone, you could have heard a pin drop. I walked right in front of the troubled teens section. Tears were coming down the faces of almost every boy. Tears began flowing from the eyes of our group. It was a moment that changed my life forever. The thought came to me as I was taking my seat that many of those boys had probably never heard those words before.

The energy felt at that moment cannot be described. It was a perfect moment that gave many of us a glimpse of what true living was really all about. I decided then that whatever I did with my life, it needed to involve helping people feel like we felt at that moment.

As we were leaving the facility that night, again we walked down the hallway towards the exit, and again the kids from the correctional facility lined both sides of the hallway. This time they were giving high fives, saying good-byes, and, yes, finishing with the words, "*I love ya, man!*"

The outer prompting said to have our group yell the words "I love ya, man." Acting on that outer prompting nourished the inner prompting that told me my purpose would have something to do with creating moments like that for people all around the world. It doesn't matter which kind of prompting you act on first; the simple action will create a positive energy flow that will guide you to abundance in your life. It is an amazingly simple way to live your potential.

INFINITE FLOW OF ENERGY

Below you will see a visual that has become known as the sign of infinity. It represents a pathway that never stops. There are no breaks or stopping points.

I like to use this symbol to represent an infinite flow of positive energy. The way to make sure the flow is positive is to make sure it is moving around positive action.

Let's take the same symbol and allow it to move around the philosophy of this book.

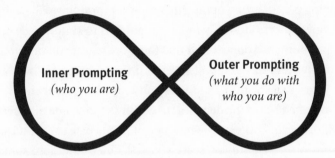

Inner Prompting
(who you are)

Outer Prompting
(what you do with who you are)

With this addition the symbol now represents an infinite flow of positive energy. With this you can envision a daily journey where you are acting on the inner promptings (who you are) and doing something with who you are by reaching out to others. This creates the ultimate balance between self and others.

You have heard it said, "It's not the destination that matters; it's the journey." If you allow this symbol to serve as your pathway, then everything becomes about the journey. Imagine the life stories collected on an infinite journey such as this. Imagine a life where you understand the philosophy of the inner and outer prompting, a life where you define who you are by acting on your inner promptings and you continuously do something with who you are by acting on your outer promptings.

WHICH COMES FIRST?

You can discover yourself simply by consistently acting positively on either type of prompting as it comes your way. It does not matter which one you start with. If you look at the infinite pathway of energy it would be safe to say you can enter it anywhere. There is no starting or stopping point. Acting upon either type of prompting will begin the energy flow process. The way to keep it going is to simply keep acting on the promptings. You will find that the more you act on promptings, the more promptings you will receive. Those promptings will guide you to your genius within, as long as you keep acting on them.

I have often heard the debate as to which should come first, serving yourself or serving others. The one side of this debate says you cannot serve someone else until you serve yourself. You cannot love someone else until you love yourself. The other side of the debate says serving yourself first is selfish. You should always focus on serving others and never worry or focus on yourself.

How about we stop the debate right now by realizing that serving self and others is best done simultaneously. Why does one have to come before the other? If you use the infinite pathway of energy as a visual, you can stay focused on the need for keeping a balance between self and others.

THE CHALLENGE

The challenge comes when there is no focus on keeping the balance. Many people get caught on one side or the other. In our seminars I have observed and worked with women who really struggle with this. By nature women are nurturers. It is in their DNA to take care of others. Some call this motherly instinct. I have actually had women laugh at me when I introduce this concept. My wife was one of them.

At one of our events I was talking to a young mother of three children about the balance between serving others and taking care of herself. The entire audience was involved with this interaction. She felt out of balance as every day was consumed with taking care of her four kids (three children and a husband). Mothers and wives often feel this way.

I asked her what she enjoyed doing. She said she loved to read. I suggested that perhaps her inner prompting might be telling her to take some alone time to read.

She laughed out loud and said, "Yeah, like that could ever happen." I asked her why she felt that could never happen. She said there is never a quiet time in her home. Every minute was filled with noise and activity. Even after the kids went to bed there were household chores to finish up. I asked her if she had ever been to a Barnes and Noble bookstore. She said, "Of course."

"Imagine two hours, by yourself, in the back corner of Barnes and Noble with a latté and a new book of your choice," I continued.

Again she laughed out loud and said, "I would love that, but I don't see me ever having the time to do that."

I asked her why.

She answered, "You are a man; you wouldn't understand." This created a stir with the rest of the audience.

I asked her again, "Would you like to be able to spend two hours alone at Barnes and Noble with your favorite book?

She said, "I would love to, but I really don't see how that would be possible."

"First of all, if you don't think it's possible, then you are right," I responded. "This is the story in your mind, and that is why you are living that reality. If you want to ever enjoy that alone time at Barnes and Noble, we will need to discover where your story came from." She agreed to participate. I then took her on a series of questions and answers that unveiled where her story had come from.

Come to find out, she had been taught growing up that her biggest responsibility in life would be to grow up, get married, and have children. She believed, as many mothers do, that her life was about taking care of her children. In her mind any activity outside of that would be selfish. Once we discovered this I asked her a very important question.

"So," I said, "you think that two hours of alone time at Barnes and Noble is not serving your children?"

"Well, no, that's only serving me," she said.

"So by getting your much-needed alone time, unwinding, recharging your mind and soul, getting the chance to relax—all of those things will not make you a better mother when you get home from the bookstore?" I asked.

She started to see where I was going, and so did the rest of the audience.

"Have you ever wondered why the safety video on the airplane instructs you to put the oxygen mask on yourself before you put it on your child?" I asked.

She said, "I always figured they did that because the adult needed to be able to breathe so she could actually take care of the child."

"Hmmm, sounds interesting," I responded. "Do you think there is a lesson in that?"

"Yeah, I guess there is," she said.

"Actually that is only one of the reasons they instruct you that way," I continued. "There is another reason. If you attempt to put that mask over the face of your child before you put it on yourself, it scares your child. They need to see you do it first so they know it is OK."

If you want your children to have confidence, take control, and be self-disciplined, they need to see their parents do it first. They need to see that it is OK to take care of yourself. It is OK to serve your needs so you can be of service to others.

In Chapter Two of this book we discussed the tennis ball exercise and how we get people to discover the old tennis balls they are hanging on to. We completed the same exercise at this event earlier in the day. This young mother concluded our discussion by saying, "I think I just discovered an old tennis ball that needs to be dropped." This was an amazing interaction that taught us all a valuable lesson that day.

My wife Jodi was at that event, and she really related with the young mother of three children. Jodi is the mother of our three beautiful children. She went through many of the same experiences this young woman had expressed. When we returned to our hotel room that night, Jodi and I had an incredible conversation about the balance between self and others.

She started by telling me she had heard me teach this before and thought for some time that I was full of ... you know what. Like the young woman at the seminar, she felt I was a man and simply did not understand. Jodi went on to say it took her several years to finally release some lifelong beliefs keeping her from taking care of herself.

Jodi was taught growing up that if you are down and things are not going right, you forget about yourself and do something for someone else. They had a family saying: "If the day be sunny, if the day be grey, if you want to be happy, give something away."

This is a true statement—as long as you have something to give away. Any time Jodi was in a bad mood or down about something, she would be reminded of this phrase and encouraged to forget about herself and go serve someone. The principle she was being taught is a true principle, but there were many times in her life she felt it did not work.

Like many, she misunderstood the principle to mean taking care of herself was bad and selfish. Serving others was the only thing she should ever do. She learned that by focusing only on others, she was out of balance, and the saying was not working for her.

The interesting thing here is that Jodi has the gift of intuition. She knows who needs help and when. She is a master at acting on the outer promptings. Always has been. Many of the principles I teach I have learned by her example. She is an amazing woman.

I have mentioned in this chapter that on the infinite pathway of positive energy, it doesn't matter where you start. That statement is true as long as you stay focused on the entire pathway.

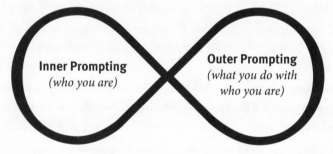

Inner Prompting
(who you are)

Outer Prompting
(what you do with who you are)

For many years Jodi was focused only on the outer-prompting side of the pathway. She was really good at acting on the outer promptings, and they were opening up the inner promptings or the voice telling her who she was. However, she would not allow herself to entertain that voice because she thought it was bad and selfish to serve herself. So here is what was happening in her life.

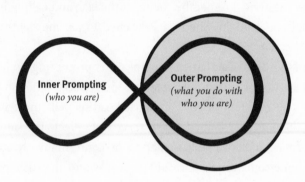

You will notice that when you focus on one side of the pathway, you end up exiting and re-entering the pathway. You stop the infinite flow. You create a new pathway that will create energy and some re-sults, but you will never be in balance. You will always feel like you are missing something.

The family saying was not working for Jodi because she did not al-low herself to stay on the infinite pathway of positive energy.

As a result she felt frustrated and did not like to be reminded of the family statement. She finally realized there might be something to all this philosophy stuff that her husband (me) was saying. She decided that, in her own way, she would take baby steps toward serving herself.

She started by picking one thing a day to do just for her. It started very small, like stopping at the gas station, getting an energy drink, and having just ten minutes to enjoy the sun shining in her face and collecting her thoughts for the day. She really enjoyed doing that. She then started reading for thirty minutes before going to bed at night. She really enjoyed that as well.

As she was discovering this side of the pathway, my two sons and I took a guys' trip for three days to Lake Powell. She had some alone time and, on her own, enrolled in a three-day seminar retreat. *Wow*! This blew me away. I remember being at the lake and calling her from my cell phone at night. She was so excited to tell me the things she learned that day.

All of these small activities were the inner promptings in Jodi's life, telling her who she was and what she needed to do to nourish herself.

Jodi tells the story of how she started getting pedicures. She really enjoyed them as they helped her to relax and reflect. The salon had a basic pedicure, a deluxe pedicure, and a pedicure/manicure combo.

For quite some time she would go and ask for the basic pedicure. It would take about thirty minutes. At first she felt a bit guilty about the time and money she was spending on this. It didn't take her long to realize how ridiculous that thought was, so she released it and enjoyed every minute of her time. She then started upgrading to the deluxe pedicure, which took forty-five minutes and included a soak, scrub, and paraffin wax on her feet. She loved every minute of that. Then she upgraded to the pedicure/manicure combo that took about two hours. Again, she loved every minute of it and did not feel one bit guilty.

As Jodi was discovering new ways to serve herself, she was also discovering who she was and was serving others in more dynamic ways. She was no longer exiting and re-entering the infinite pathway of energy. She was now flowing between the inner- and outer-prompting journey.

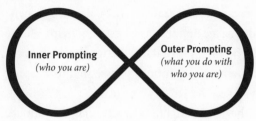

THE "AHA" MOMENT

At one of her pedicure appointments Jodi had a real "aha" moment. An older woman on oxygen walked into the salon. She was with a younger woman, her daughter. Jodi watched as they both received a pedicure. She noticed how much the older woman enjoyed it. She noticed how grateful the older woman was to her daughter for bringing her there and to the woman who was providing such an amazing service.

Jodi watched this and realized it probably took this old woman a lifetime to figure out it was OK to be pampered and taken care of. It was OK to take care of herself. She also thought that paying for two pedicures might be a stretch for the young daughter.

Acting on a prompting, Jodi paid their bill and asked for it to remain anonymous. When the mother and daughter went to leave, the patrons of the salon told them the bill had already been paid. The daughter could not believe it. In fact, she insisted that her bill had not been paid and could not imagine anyone would do this for them.

Jodi watched this interaction. She noticed the daughter was a nurturer. She was caring for her ailing mother. It was hard for this daughter to receive an act of kindness because she was so busy giving acts of kindness. This is what Jodi had been caught up in for so many years. Jodi decided then and there that she would be more accepting of other people's acts of service. She realized that balance between self and others also includes accepting the flow between giving and receiving. She learned those who maintain balance between self and others are givers *and* receivers. Being good at both is essential to keeping the infinite flow of energy alive.

As the mother and daughter were leaving, they looked around the salon to see if they could figure out who had done this for them. Jodi looked down at her newly pedicured feet and smiled.

The woman at the seminar and my wife Jodi went through a phase where they were out of balance on the outer-prompting or serving-others side of the pathway. There are many who might be out of balance on the side of serving themselves.

You can take the same infinite pathway illustration and see what happens on the other side. You will notice that Jodi exited the pathway on the outer-prompting side and interrupted the balancing flow of energy. Those caught up in self would look like this.

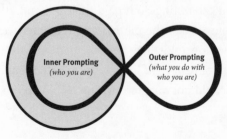

This usually starts as a good intention, with individuals who want to discover their uniqueness. They diligently search for and work on their gifts and talents so they can improve their quality of life. Again, entering the infinite pathway on the inner-prompting side is great as long as you stay focused on the entire pathway.

As we move along our journey of personal development, it can be easy to stray from that pathway. As the illustration shows, by exiting the pathway you create a new energy flow; it will get you results, but you will not be in balance.

There are three types of people attracting three very different types of results

You will actually find yourself in one of three categories at various times of your life. Two of them are out of balance. One is in balance. If you simply visualize this process, you can see when you are getting out of balance and correct yourself. You can also quickly see what you are sending out and attracting.

1— The I/Me Person

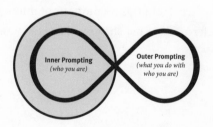

I/Me Person: These are people who live for themselves and through themselves. Self-absorbed. Self-centered. Out of balance.

Law of Attraction: The **I/Me** person sends out to himself and to others that he is superior to, better than, more worthy than, and doesn't have time for others. What people receive from this is feelings of inferiority or unworthiness. The **I/Me** then attracts inferiority. What he gives is what he attracts.

2— The You/You Person

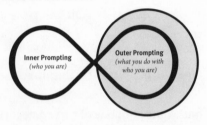

You/You: This is someone who lives for others and through others. Co-dependent. Out of balance.

Law of Attraction: The **You/You** person sends out to herself that she is inferior to others and undeserving of the good things in life. She sends this because she has lost focus of herself or failed to care for herself. What she receives from this is emotions of inferiority. The **you/you** then attracts inferiority. What she gives is what she attracts.

1— The I/We Person

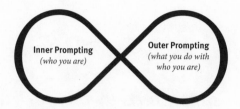

I/We: These are people who live for themselves through others. In balance between self and others.

Law of Attraction: The **I/We** person sends out that she is on equal ground, we are all good, and we are all deserving. She knows what she stands for. What people receive from this are the emotions of acceptance, confidence, and love. What she gives is what she attracts.

BALANCE BETWEEN SELF AND OTHERS

To simplify this balancing philosophy, we simply focus on the basic fundamental upon which it is built. The inner prompting is who you are, and the outer prompting is what you do with who you are. If you build an infinite pathway around those two things, you will create an infinite flow of positive energy that will guide you to abundance throughout your life.

Remember, it is not about the destination; it is about the journey. It's about the stories you collect along the way. If your pathway intertwines between the inner and outer promptings, you will collect some amazing stories throughout your life.

"The day of the 'go-getter' has passed. He has been supplanted by the 'go- giver'."

NAPOLEON HILL

"Do all the good you can in all the ways you can in all the places you can at all times you can to all the people you can as long as ever you can."

JOHN WESLEY

CHAPTER 8

Sending Out to Give

When I was growing up, my mom always told me I was meant to do something special in the world. Every time she said that, she would follow up by saying, "Son, you have gifts, and you were meant to give them away." It took me a while to figure out exactly what she meant.

It wasn't the speeches she gave me or the stories she told that taught me what she meant. It was the way she lived her life. My mom gave birth to seven children. Mom and Dad adopted four more children after that. That is a total of eleven children, and I am happy to report that I was her favorite.

The funny part of that claim is that all eleven children felt they were Mom's favorite. That was her gift. She had this amazing ability to make everyone feel as if they were her favorite—her children, her friends, those she worked with. Everyone felt they were Mom's favorite.

Mom was always the center of attention. She loved having people around her, and she lived each moment to the fullest. She believed everyone had uniqueness and that when they found their uniqueness, they would live happily ever after by giving their uniqueness away. Again, she taught by her example far more than by her words.

Mom believed that nourishment to the mind, the body, the heart, and the soul were the keys to happy living. She was an amazing provider of nourishment in all those areas. She loved to cook and, boy, could she cook. I remember growing up in a home that always had fresh baked homemade bread with bottled homemade jam. She made cinnamon rolls that were out of this world.

One of my favorite treats was her bottled peaches and pears. Every summer she would go on a bottling frenzy. She invited friends and family over to participate, and it was a big summer party. My dad would always plant a big garden with fresh tomatoes, cucumbers, corn, beans, squash, and any other vegetable he could fit into the garden. The kids would weed and water that garden and prepare it for harvest time. My mom loved harvest time. From the first tomato off the plant in late June to baskets full of vegetables and fruits in late August, everything that came from the garden was something for Mom to celebrate. She used to take fresh squash, dip it in her own batter recipe, and fry it up in a pan. Neighbors, friends, and extended family would come out of the woodwork when Mom was serving fried squash.

I grew up in a large home positioned on a street corner all the neighbors drove by. As I was growing up my folks kept building onto the home. We ended up with an indoor swimming pool, a large garden room, and a game room with a pool table. My mom always liked the idea of having a large home because she saw it as a place where family and friends could come and enjoy each other's company. The doors of our home were open to everyone. My mother made sure of it.

Mom passed away about one year prior to this writing. I miss my mom. She taught me some of the most valuable lessons in life. She taught me to believe in myself. She taught me to dream big because I was destined for greatness. She taught me how to live a life of giving. She expected it.

One of the things Mom always told me was that I had a gift for music. I believed everything my mom said. Fortunately for me, Mom pointed out my gifts and talents, and I believed in her words. She helped me from a very early age to create positive stories in my mind about myself. I always loved to write. Growing up I would write poems and short stories. Mom told me I was a great writer and had the ability to influence many for good. I believed her.

When Mom died, I decided to pay tribute to her by combining what she always told me were two of my gifts—music and writing. I wrote a song that shared with others what my mom was all about. The song is titled "Send to Give."

"SEND TO GIVE"

Mama always said, Be nice and have fun, keep a smile on your face, and find the good in everyone.

She would say people need a place to call home, no one ever wants to feel alone.

The time is now, a time to give, reaching out is the only way to live.

Let it happen, you can give it away (send to give), living life for a brighter day.

My Mama is gone, her message lives on, and we feel her presence when we're singing this song.

*I'm gonna be finding, I'm gonna keep rising, I'm gonna
   keep shining, and all I got to do is believe, to send,
   believe, to give, sending to give yeah, all I gotta do is
   believe, to send, believe, to give, sending to give yeah …
   now everybody's sending to give.*

*Mama used to say, know that you could be the very best,
   understanding how to pass the test.*

*Never putting you beneath or above, you and I, other
   people we're all equal in love.*

*The time is now, a time to give, reaching out is the only
   way to live.*

*Let it happen, you can give it away, send to give, living
   life for a brighter day.*

*My Mama is gone, her message lives on, and we feel her
   presence when were singing this song.*

*I'm gonna be finding, I'm gonna keep rising, I'm gonna
   keep shining, and all I got to do is believe, to send,
   believe, to give, sending to give yeah, all I gotta do is
   believe, to send, believe, to give, sending to give yeah …
   now everybody's sending to give.*

*There are things in life that only you can do, remember
   that applies to others too.*

*It's time to check our egos when we get to the door, enter
   in and see there's so much more.*

*The time is now for you and me, send to give is our
   philosophy.*

*Let it happen, you can give it away, living life for a
   brighter day.*

*My Mama is gone, her message lives on, and we feel her
   presence when we're singing this song.*

*I'm gonna be finding, I'm gonna keep rising, I'm gonna
keep shining, and all I got to do is believe, to send,
believe, to give, sending to give yeah, all I gotta do is
believe, to send, believe, to give, sending to give yeah ...
now everybody's sending to give.*
Now everybody's sending to give.

The lyrics of this song portray the philosophy that my mother lived by. She was a very simple person who loved people. She was always giving, and she always had so much to give. For the majority of her life, she was the perfect example of maintaining a balance between self and others. She knew who she was, and she gave herself away.

Let's explore the lyrics of this song:

"Mama always said, 'Be nice and have fun. Keep a smile on your face, and find the good in everyone.

It was important to my mom that you were nice to yourself and to others at all times. When she saw her kids feeling discouraged, she would remind us of who we were—someone special. She didn't put up with a whole lot of whining. She would lovingly remind us of our uniqueness, and then give us a swift kick in the butt if we kept belly-aching. She was not a fan of sulking or frowning. She always had a way of putting a smile on our faces. There was not much time in our home for feeling sorry for ourselves. Mom didn't put up with it.

Mom was a master at finding the good in others. I remember her telling me that if I found the good in myself, it would always be easy for me to find the good in others. I always knew my mom knew the good she had in herself because she was so good at finding it in others.

"She would say people need a place to call home. No one ever wants to feel alone."

I already mentioned that Mom opened her doors to everyone. Our home was like the community recreation center growing up. Everyone felt welcome. To this day I still run around with a childhood friend named Dave Smith. Dave grew up in my home. He was always there. He remembers the same stories about the homemade bread and the swift kicks in the butt when we needed them. He remembers being treated like one of the family.

"Mama used to say, 'Know that you can be the very best, understanding how to pass the test.'"

Mom celebrated people's uniqueness. She believed everyone had something unique to offer the world. She was really good at helping people find their gifts. That was one of the reasons everyone felt they were her favorite person. During the one-on-one moments spent with her, you were her favorite because she celebrated who you were. To Mom, passing the test of life was nothing more than finding who you are and then giving yourself away.

"Never putting you beneath or above—you and I, other people, we're all equal in love."

Mom believed everyone was special in his or her own way. She had very little patience for anyone that mistreated another human being, and she didn't like it when people mistreated themselves either. And let me tell you, even if she didn't know you well, she would let you know about it if you crossed those lines. I remember a time when my brother Kris was in a high school wrestling match. I was in the stands sitting next to my mom and dad. Kris had twisted his knee in the match but insisted that he finish. They took a timeout to wrap his knee. Someone sitting in the stands about five rows below us started yelling, "Go for the knee, go for the knee."

Wow! Wrong thing to say. My mom flew over the top of me and was down those five rows in record time. One thing you did not mess with, and that was one of my mom's kids. There was fear in the eyes of that person, and he was very apologetic. I will never forget the way she stood up for Kris. I watched her do that for many people through the years. You never put yourself beneath or above another. She would have none of it.

She believed love was the great equalizer of all people. Again, she lived that message far more than she ever spoke it.

"There are things in life that only you can do; remember, that applies to others too."

You have already read many examples about how my mother believed this, not only about herself and her children, but about everyone. It was very important to her that you recognized your special gifts and the gifts of others. Everyone's life deserved celebration with my mom.

"It's time to check our egos when we get to the door; enter in and see there's so much more."

Mom knew keeping a balance between self and others would keep a person humble and real. With ego out of the way we can live the special moments of life—moments of celebration where we can learn from and enjoy each other because we are not worried about being better than anyone else.

"The time is now—a time to give; reaching out is the only way to live. Let it happen, you can give it away (send to give), living life for a brighter day."

Whenever Mom sent a message to anyone, it was in the spirit of giving. She gave for the sake of giving. She was not the type to wonder what she might receive after giving of herself. She simply gave to give. I believe this is a valuable philosophy to live by. Especially today.

People are reaching out more today than they ever have. Technology has made our world a much smaller place. National boundaries and barriers have come down. Advanced education and exposure to different cultures, ethnicities, and groups of people have brought us closer as people. Social networking websites like MySpace, Facebook, and Twitter have helped us connect with other human beings around the world.

Modern technology has brought back the power of pictures, gifts, and the written word. Programs like SendOutCards allow you to use technology to send a physical greeting card with pictures and messages of celebration. We live in a day and age where you can do a quick Internet search on any product or service and have access to hundreds of options in just seconds. Today more than ever, there is a need to genuinely connect with people in your business ventures. People today are concerned less and less about what you are offering and more and more that you actually care.

Phrases like "relationship marketing" are taking on a whole new meaning as these technologies allow us to make genuine connections with others. Appreciation wins over self-promotion every single time, especially today. My good friends Tommy Wyatt and Curtis Lewsey wrote a book titled *Appreciation Marketing*. This amazing book explains the value of "giving to give" in your business and your personal life.

GOLDEN QUESTION

The golden question today is this: Whenever you are sending anything out, to yourself or to others through your thoughts, feelings, words, or deeds, are you sending to get, or are you sending to give?

Laws of Attraction state that if you are sending to get, then the universe gets or keeps. In other words, it will pull away from you that which you desire.

If you are sending to give, then the universe gives back. In other words, it draws to you that which you desire.

Speaking of the golden question, just a few minutes before I typed these words, Jodi and I made a phone call to a dear friend, Bob Golden, on his birthday. Our family sang him "Happy Birthday." When we finished, he said he thought that I would have sung him a rap for his birthday, as I am known to many as Kody B, the master MC.

I rattled off a freestyle rhyme that went something like this.

> *Yo... Yo... we bustin' birthday wishes to Bobby G.*
> *Comin' from Kody B, the master MC.*
> *You know it's time to celebrate*
> *The birthday of the man that defined great.*
> *Bobby G, the man with the plan*
> *Changing the world with his great "I am's."*

True story, that was on-the-spot freestyle right over the phone.

I share this because of the person we celebrated. You cannot mention Bob Golden without also mentioning his wife Betty Ann. They are an amazing team that gives to give every day of their lives. I am inspired by their commitment to celebrating others.

In wishing Bob his happy birthday he was very quick to shift the attention from himself to everyone around him. He said he and Betty

Ann felt blessed to be associated with us. He felt blessed that they had the opportunity to celebrate the birthdays of everyone around them. He said that every day is a birthday to someone, so every day is a special day.

Bob and Betty Ann have built lifelong relationships around the world with their giving attitude. They have also built a multi-million-dollar in-home business by celebrating people on their birthdays and at unexpected times. They don't do those things to build their business. They do them to celebrate the lives of people they meet. As a result, they have had thousands of people join them in their business because people know that the Goldens care.

Sending to give represents a philosophy that generates the highest level of positive energy. I am reminded of a poem I wrote in my journal several years ago, titled "Sending Out Your Best." It goes like this:

Care for your brothers
Cherish your friends
Celebrate a life before a life is taken
Be quick to make amends

Do unto others as the saying goes
Send out what you wish to receive
Success is determined by who you are
And that which you choose to believe

You can send out the best or send out the worst
Through thoughts, through words and deeds
It's the feelings you send that count the most
It's caring for someone's needs

There's a need to feel appreciated
A need to know people care
Deliver these things to those in your life
And receive them beyond compare

So send out the best and dare to dream
What you ask for you will receive
It's time to make the difference you can
Your wishes you will achieve

Children of all ages want parents to be proud
Friends want friends to accept
Every spouse wants to know they are loved
Every person wants to connect

The lost art of writing is what we need
So feelings might be expressed
Messages within we cannot speak
Hearts waiting to be impressed

If you love 'em—tell 'em
If you care—then share
If you are prompted—act
If you have hope—then give

Life is available in abundance
Dreams are meant to be real
It's not what you say or what you do
It's how you make them feel

Today is the day for you to begin
Be who you were meant to be
Happily ever after is real
It's you sending good to me

You deserve exactly what you send out, so send all the good you can to the world. And, yes, your hopes and dreams will come true.

Bon Jovi sings a song titled, "Welcome to Wherever You Are." One line in this song says, "Maybe we are all different, but we're all still the same."

I believe this is a profound line with lots of meaning. I believe we are all different in that everyone has different values, beliefs, and personality windows. The following boxes illustrate how value, belief and personality windows work.

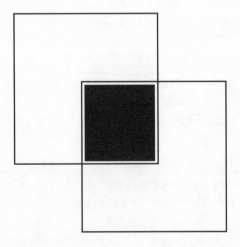

Let's say that the top left box represents you and the bottom right window represents your spouse or someone close to you. In the middle, where it is shaded, your window perfectly aligns with the window of the other person. This is where you think, feel, and act the same way. You laugh at the same jokes, enjoy some of the same hobbies, and share some the same philosophies.

The top right section of the upper box (you) is where you think, feel, and act totally different from the person close to you. Down in the bottom right section of the lower box (other person) is where that person thinks, feels, and acts totally different than you. How much time do we spend trying to perfectly align our value and belief windows with others in our life? The sad thing about doing this is that it will never happen, so why do we try? This is a tremendous waste of energy. In fact, it blocks us from the energy that comes from true giving. Those boxes represent how we are all different.

If you are trying to get another person's value and belief window to match yours, will you be sending out to get from that person or sending out to give? The answer is obvious. If you are trying to *get* someone to do something, you are sending out to *get*.

Rather than focusing on how we are different from others, we can simply focus on how we are all the same. We are the same, in that we all have a desire to love and be loved. In fact, in the end that's all there is. Love is the great equalizer that brings differences together. The following circles illustrate how the desire to love and be loved works.

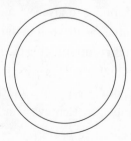

You can see that the two circles are in perfect alignment. There is no need to shift anything. You have a desire to love and be loved, your spouse or someone close to you has the desire to love and be loved, and if you celebrate that great commonality, you will be sending out to give to that person and to everyone around you.

Focusing on the circles (the desire to love and be loved) allows me to celebrate my differences with others. This is how the barriers of race, color, creed, nationality, lifestyle, and even religion are broken down. This allows me to celebrate my differences with others while respecting them for who they are. It creates diversity and variety in my life.

Some of my closest friends in all the world come from vastly different backgrounds and beliefs than I do. I have learned so much from each of them. They respect me for who I am, and I respect them for who they are. At the end of the day all of us are brothers and sisters in this game called *Life*, and through a constant state of giving to give we can live life more abundantly.

In his book *The Power of Intention*, Wayne Dyer tells us that "research has shown that a simple act of kindness directed toward another improves the functioning of the immune system and stimulates the production of serotonin (the feel-good chemical in our brain) in both the recipient of the kindness and the person extending the kindness. Even more amazing is that persons observing the act of kindness have similar beneficial results."

It sounds to me like we were built to reach out in kindness to others. It is in our DNA. Sending to give is a message for the ages and a philosophy that is essential for survival in today's world.

Being a Christian, I grew up studying the Bible. The Bible is a foundational book of scripture that guides my spiritual and personal development. The word "succour" shows up a few times in the Old and New Testament. As an example, in Hebrews, Chapter 2, Verse 18 it says,

"For in that he himself (Jesus) hath suffered being tempted, he is able to succour them that are tempted."

I learned that the word "succour" means "to run to." When that word is used, it implies that Jesus runs to those who are tempted. He runs to those who are in need. He runs to wipe the tears of a troubled soul. He runs to comfort those that stand in need of comfort. He runs to give love to all. In the spirit of giving to give, may we follow this example and run to those who can benefit from who we are.

The movie *Saving Private Ryan* contains a scene where a captain saves the life of Private Ryan and, as a result, is about to die himself. Private Ryan asks the dying captain his final question: "How can I ever repay you?" With his dying words the captain answers, "Just make it worth it."

Put yourself in the shoes of Private Ryan. How would you deliver on that request? How would you make it worth it to continue your life after someone died for you? I believe the answer has been made clear in this chapter. Find out who you are and then give yourself away. Give for the sake of giving and celebrate the lives of everyone around you.

"Treat everyone you meet, friend or foe, loved one or stranger, as if they were going to be dead at midnight."

OG MANDINO

"Act like you like somebody and pretty soon you will."

PERRY KASSING

CHAPTER 9

Celebrate Life Now

When I was twelve years old, I attended my first funeral. I remember it well because it was for the mother of my friend Jim Sorensen. I knew Jim's mom because I had spent time in his home. His mother used to fix us sandwiches and lemonade. She was a really nice lady. Once the doctors discovered she had cancer, it wasn't long before she passed away.

What I remember most about the funeral was all the amazing things everyone was saying about Jim's mom. I overheard people in conversation as they were waiting for the funeral to start. Everyone I heard was celebrating the life of this woman. They were sad, but they were sharing stories of joy and accomplishment in the life of this amazing lady.

When the funeral program began, the speakers got up and, again, started telling amazing stories about this lady. As a twelve-year-old boy I remember thinking, *Why did we wait for Jim's mother to die before we said all these nice things about her? I sure wish she was here right now because I want to thank her for always being so nice to me.*

Many things have happened in my life since attending my first funeral, and there have been many funerals since. I have attended funerals for grandmas, grandpas, extended family members, friends, and of course my brother Kris and my mother. Every time I attended these funerals, the same thing happened. All the kind things were said to celebrate the person lying in the casket, and I wondered why we didn't say these things when they were alive.

After losing my brother and learning the lesson about promptings, I have vowed to celebrate people while they are living. We have created systems and technologies that allow us to quickly act on promptings and celebrate people while they are here.

At SendOutCards we celebrate life with pictures, gifts, and the written word. I have made a commitment to send at least one heartfelt greeting card every day to people in my life. I also remember birthdays and special occasions and celebrate people on their special day. Everyone feels different on their birthday. It is a special day, and we all crave the recognition we deserve on our birthdays. I have challenged hundreds of thousands of others to make this same commitment, to celebrate life now. Millions of greeting cards and gifts are being sent through our system every year. One of the greatest joys of my day is to walk out to our print shop where thousands of heartfelt cards are being printed. Incredible pictures have been captured and are displayed on these cards. Creative captions and word bubbles add humor and meaning to these pictures, and a person's life is being celebrated.

People love to see pictures of themselves. Anyone who denies this is lying. In fact, if you know anyone who says he doesn't like pictures of himself, I would submit the following challenge: With that person nearby, get your digital camera out and start scrolling through your pictures. If that person knows you have pictures of him, where do you think he will be? He'll be looking over your shoulder, waiting for his picture to show up.

Pictures and the written word are great ways to celebrate others. We use greeting cards to get that celebration out to the living. Adding gifts is another way to let people know you care about and appreciate them.

FLAT TIRE ON THE SIDE OF THE STREET

My friend Matthew Mortensen tells the story about a teenage boy we both worked with in church youth programs. Matthew was driving home from work one evening and noticed the boy, Nick Wanless, on the side of the street fixing a flat tire. As Matthew was driving by he had a prompting to pull over and help Nick and his buddy with the flat tire. He ignored the prompting as he was in a hurry to get home.

The boys fixed that tire. A few hours later they were driving on a two-lane highway, attempted to pass another vehicle, and went head-on with a car coming from the other direction. Nick and his friend died at the scene of this accident. When Matthew got the news of the accident, he was devastated. He had ignored a prompting to help his friend Nick and would never have the opportunity to do it again. Sound familiar?

To this day Matthew cannot tell that story without getting choked up. He always mentions that had he known Nick was about to die, he would have moved the world to pull over and help him fix the flat tire. This reminds me of the quote by Og Mandino: "Treat everyone you know as if they were going to be dead at midnight." This may sound like a morbid thought, but it is powerful. If we followed that advice, imagine the way in which we would celebrate everyone that comes our way.

As I mentioned, Nick was a young man I knew and worked with at church. He was a great kid. When I received news of the accident, I went into my account at SendOutCards, looked up his name, and saw that I had sent him five greeting cards over the last two years. I remembered Nick on two of his birthdays, I sent him a "job well done" card after he gave a talk in church, and I sent him a card highlighting a youth activity we had gone on together. I had celebrated Nick while he was alive. He knew that I cared.

WHEN THE PROMPTING COMES, ACT!

Several years ago a gentleman named Bob Martin attended several of our seminars. He was an associate in our business and an amazing greeting card sender. At one particular event Bob asked if I would step outside for a moment. We walked out the front door, and Bob tearfully told me the following story:

> *"When I moved here to Salt Lake City in 1974, I went into real estate. I hired on with Ken Evans Realty with the help of Steve Evans' recommendation. I had met Steve my first afternoon in town. Steve Evans became an unofficial mentor of sorts. I worked with him as a shadow on several occasions early on in my real estate career and learned much from him. Currently I am a business coach and coach many Realtors on how to improve their business. I draw on my experiences with Steve often. During the course of this coaching I realized perhaps more than ever before the part Steve played in my business success and my life. He was a real force in the development of my faith and in my life in general.*
>
> *As happens too often to all of us, I suppose, Steve and I drifted apart—busy with life, working for different real-estate companies. Why is it in our lives we have room for those people immediately around us*

but often lose touch with those most important to us, merely because it requires a little effort since they are no longer an everyday visitor to our circle?

In March of 2004 I felt impressed to contact my mentor in real estate, Steve Evans. I talked with Steve by phone, and we scheduled a time to get together at his home. At various times both of us had to reschedule, and by May 2004, when I attended your seminar, Steve and I had still not gotten together. During the seminar that day you asked us to think of a person that meant something to us and send him or her a greeting card. I chose Steve Evans. I couldn't seem to get my thoughts together that day and so vowed to work on it more after the seminar. I did work on it more but still felt I did not say all I wanted to say. I felt blocked—time began to drift away. Still I had not sent the card to Steve—I wanted it to be perfect.

Then one day in August I was reading the Sunday paper. I saw Steve's picture. He had died unexpectedly on August 19, 2004. I knew he had suffered an injury in a fall years earlier but this—how could this be! And still I had not sent my card! I looked around my home office—there on the floor to the left of my desk lay my latest draft of the card I never sent to Steve. I was crushed, more than I could have imagined! How sad, I thought. I cried openly.

I attended his funeral and heard the accolades and silently mourned for what might have been. A card I should have sent, a dear friend that meant more to me than I ever let on, and a friendship that

could have been so much more than it was. Time,
inconvenience and being too busy with the business
of life to acknowledge one of life's greatest blessings—
a friend for the ages—prevented me from sending the
card until it was too late."

Bob learned the same lesson with this experience that I had learned through the death of my brother. When the prompting comes, we must act. The promptings show up for a reason. They are given to us to see if we will celebrate the person we were prompted to reach out to.

CELEBRATE LIFE THROUGH PROMPTINGS AND LIVE A LIFE OF CELEBRATION

We have said many times that the outer prompting is what you do with who you are. It's reaching out in kindness and generosity to others. It's celebrating a life before a life is taken. We have also talked about getting to Level Four with good habits. If you remember, Level Four is where you no longer think about an activity; you just do it.

Fortunately, I have gotten to Level Four with sending heartfelt greeting cards every day. This is one of the reasons Nick Wanless received five greeting cards from me in the final two years of his life. One of the things I do is send a greeting card to the first person that comes to my mind every morning. This is how I start my day. It's an amazing way to begin a day because it helps you to always start on a positive note.

We have mentioned that close to 90 percent of everything you are exposed to in a given day is negative. Because of this we need activities that help us dramatically bring that exposure down. By sending a heartfelt card I immediately flush any negative I have. You cannot share kindness from your heart to another person and think a negative thought at the same time. Try it. It is not possible.

By starting my day this way there are four things happening to further my personal development:

- I flush out the negative
- I replace it with positive
- I send out the positives to others
- What I am sending I receive tenfold in my life

By the simple act of acting daily on promptings with greeting cards, I have those four things going for me. Since I developed this habit I have sent thousands of cards and attracted a life of happiness and abundance. Why? Because every day I am celebrating the life of another human being. What you send out is what you get back. What I am getting back is my own life being celebrated. I have my set of ongoing challenges, just like everyone, but there is not a morning I wake up that I'm not excited to be alive.

MUSIC AT THE CHURCH

Every seminar I give I tell this story because it helps us understand the power of a prompting and the importance of celebrating life now.

As mentioned, I am a Level Four card sender. I no longer think about it; I just do it. I got up on a bright Saturday morning, jumped in my truck, and was heading to the office. The first person that came to mind was a lady by the name of Pat Chase. Pat takes care of the music at the church I attend. *Cool*, I thought, *when I get to the office I will send Pat a card*. I got to the office, immediately opened up my greeting card system, and looked up Pat Chase. I already had her name and address saved along with about 1,700 other names and addresses at the time. I went to the online greeting card catalog, went to the motivational section, and found a card that said, "Beauty" on the front. The inside right of the card said, "Things are beautiful if you love them." This was the perfect greeting card.

I typed a message on the left panel saying:

> Pat,
> Just a quick note to let you know I appreciate all
> you do for us at the church. You make music beauti-
> ful, and I am a better person for it.
> Your Friend,
> Kody

Then I simply pushed the send button. This sent that card over the Internet to our printers, where thousands of cards just like it are printed, stuffed, stamped, and mailed every day.

It took me thirty-seven seconds to send that card. Talk about acting on a prompting. The thing I love about the SendOutCards program is that it allows you to act on your promptings just like this every day.

About two weeks went by. I showed up at church, and Pat Chase walked up to me. She said, "Kody, can I speak to you?" We stepped over to a corner where she told me the following story.

"First of all, I would like to thank you for the card you sent me," she began.

"You are very welcome, Pat, and I want you to know I really meant it," I said. "My life is blessed with the beautiful music you provide."

"I would like to tell you what happened the day I received that card," Pat said. "It was a Thursday morning. I woke up feeling really discouraged and down, especially about my assignment at the church. You know, I don't remember the last time someone thanked me for what I was doing. In fact, the only thing I could remember were the complaints. I walked into my front room that morning and picked up the receiver of my phone. I began to dial the number of the church leader. I was about to let him know that I would no longer be doing the music at the church. But something told me to hang up the phone and walk out to get the mail first. So I hung up the phone, walked out to the mailbox, and the only piece of mail in that mailbox was a greeting card from you. I opened the card, read it, and openly wept at the mailbox."

Her final words were priceless. She said, "Kody, thank you so much for that greeting card. I will never forget you for how you made me feel on that day."

This kind of thing is going on thousands of times every day through the SendOutCards service. This is celebration of the living in its finest and simplest form. I am thankful for the opportunity to participate in this every day. I think it is safe to say thousands of people are delivering on a promise I made to my brother Kris so many years ago—a promise that I would act on my promptings and help others do the same.

CELEBRATING LIFE IS MORE THAN JUST A THANK YOU

I am amazed at the everyday miracles people perform—the single mom who takes care of her three little children while holding down a full-time job; the young student who works half the night and goes to college all day, determined to get his degree; the father who works all day, coaches his kids' baseball team three nights a week, and always manages to take his wife out on the Friday-night date.

We could go on with everyday examples like this all day long. The bottom line is there are things in life that you have done or are doing that you deserve a standing ovation for. Pat Chase may never get the awards banquet she deserves, but I can promise you one thing: She deserves that standing ovation for the lives she has blessed with her music.

I encourage everyone reading these words to be a "stand-on-your-feet- and-cheer-each-other-on" kind of people.

A few years ago, a story in *Reader's Digest* told about a woman named Lauren Manning, who was running late one morning. She had a baby boy to care for and a job to get to and not enough time to do it. She finally made it to work, but she was about thirty minutes late. She rushed into Tower 1 of the World Trade Center in New York City on that fateful morning of September 11, 2001. Little did she know a plane had already hit the building she had entered.

Lauren made it to the elevator but only in time to be doused with jet fuel that was running down the elevator shaft. There was an explosion that forced her through some metal doors, and as her hands hit those doors, they were severely burned. She made it outside but not before her body was consumed in flames. Lauren was one of the first victims taken by ambulance to a nearby hospital. She was saved, but 82 percent of her body had been severely burned. The worst damage was done to her hands.

Her husband Greg feared she was dead but later found her at the hospital. She told him she was determined to survive for him and their baby boy. Since this time there have been many stories written about Lauren and her painful road to recovery. Her husband wrote a collection of heartbreaking emails to family and friends documenting her day-to-day battle. They were compiled in a bestselling book, *Love, Greg & Lauren*.

Of the many stories that followed, one really stuck out for me. It was the time she spoke at her firm's Central Park memorial on the anniversary of 9/11. She asked families and friends to clap instead of standing for a moment of prayer. "I want to clap until my arms ache," she told them, "to make so much noise that God can hear us...that we celebrate the time we had with them." The applause was thunderous. She also quoted from a favorite William Wordsworth poem that comforts her: "We will grieve not, rather find strength in what remains behind...."

Since reading this story I have been inspired to use my healthy and strong hands to clap and cheer for lives needing to be celebrated. I have chosen not to take my ability to applaud others for granted. Lauren encouraged her co-workers that day to stand and cheer for those who perished. Through the Wordsworth poem she also encouraged them to cheer for all who survived.

I have had many opportunities in public settings to pay tribute to someone who has passed away, and this is how I now choose to pay such a tribute. I will say, "Normally when we honor a fallen brother or sister, we have a moment of silence. Today I would ask that we stand and cheer for this person because he lived a life deserving of a standing ovation." People always stand with thunderous applause. I even take this a step further, saying we should stand and cheer for those who survived—loved ones and friends alike. We are survivors. Every day we wake up and collect stories along life's pathway; we are survivors, deserving of a better tomorrow.

SURVIVORS

Many of us have read and watched movies about the Titanic, the unsinkable ship. The history books taught us it *was* sinkable, for on that fateful day—April 15, 1912—after running into an iceberg in the chilling ocean waters, the Titanic sank, and 1,517 people died.

Yes, this was an enormous tragedy, the single biggest loss of life in the history of civilian ocean travel. What we hear less about is the miracle part of this story: that 706 people survived. Any time a human life is saved, it is a miracle.

I share this story because on my wrist is a watch built from the remains of the Titanic. The round frame around the facing is built from rusted metal pulled from the ship. The surface of the watch rests under glass as most watches do. But the surface of this watch is made with processed coal pulled from the wreckage. This provides a crystal black surface, especially beautiful when the sunlight shines on it.

I tell you the story of this watch for two reasons. The first reason is because the watch represents survivors. Every time I wear this watch I think of survivors. I think of the value of human life.

The second reason is because of the person who gave me this watch. You see, this watch was a gift, a very expensive gift from a person who knows the value of celebrating life now. In fact, he is a master at it. This is an individual who has created a balance between his inner and outer promptings, a person who gives to give. Every time I wear this watch I not only think of survivors and the value of human life, but I also think of the person who gave it to me. As a look down at this timepiece, I know it represents greatness in humanity.

Jordan Adler is the man who gave me this watch on my forty-fifth birthday. He did it because he chose to celebrate me. He knew I loved stories and would proudly walk around telling people the story behind the watch.

Jordan lives by a motto and encourages everyone he meets to follow it too. He will tell you the motto is only four words long, simple to remember and to live by. The motto is *"Be generous every day."* He goes on to explain how important it is to be generous to yourself and to others every day of your life. Like my mother, Jordan teaches by example.

I encourage everyone to live by this simple four-word motto: *"Be generous every day."* Be generous to yourself by acting on your inner promptings every day. Be generous to others by acting on your outer promptings every day. Celebrate life now, including your own life, and live a life of abundance.

"*In nature, there are neither rewards nor punishments. There are consequences.*"

ROBERT GREENE INGERSOLL

"*I have found that if you love life, life will love you back.*"

ARTUR RUBINSTEIN

CHAPTER 10

What You Send Out is
What You Get Back

Every morning I have the opportunity to sit down at my computer and send cards to people I care about. Many of those cards are unexpected, heartfelt cards; many of them are birthday cards. It's a blessing to have a system that never lets you forget a birthday. There are days that my reminder list will have one birthday; other days there might be ten. It is a great joy to start each day sending pictures and words of celebration to others.

On one such morning I was reminded that my good friend Sid Garrett's birthday was coming up. I sat back and thought for a moment about Sid—memories of us snowmobiling together, helping each other with home improvement projects, going to dinner with our families together. He is a great friend—the type who is always there for you. He is certainly a person whose life is worth celebrating.

I spent a little extra time finding just the right birthday card. I noticed we had lots of funny new ones. I found just the right card and typed a heartfelt message in my own handwriting. I signed my name, chose blue ink, added a $25 restaurant gift card, and pushed the send button. Wow! What an incredible experience. This simple activity is one I do every day. It puts me into a positive vibrational field of energy, and it always works. With that energy I am able to stay in a "send out to give" mindset, act on my promptings, and enjoy consistent guidance toward the genius I have to offer the world.

You can read about the Law of Attraction, you can listen to tapes and watch videos about the Law of Attraction, you can continually learn about its universal laws and how you attract exactly what you send out. I do all of those things, and I even teach courses and seminars on its principles. But until you consistently do something every day to trigger the positives in your life, you will only be learning, not doing.

I am grateful I have a system that allows me to remember and celebrate those around me. We all know that what you send out in life is what you receive. As I send cards every day, I receive cards every day. I don't always get those cards from people I sent them to, but I always receive cards every day. So now each day starts with sending cards out and reading cards that came in. The positive energy created each day by writing and reading cards cannot be matched by any other activity I know of. The best part is that it never gets old. I am as excited by sending my 9,000th card as I was by sending my very first card. In fact, I get more excited with each card sent. The same thing applies to cards I receive. I love to sit and read them; they nourish my soul and give me the encouragement I need to do miraculous things in the world.

I would like to share a story about a SendOutCards user who had a magical experience on Thanksgiving Day.

Tammy Tewalt is from Sisters, Oregon. She is in the habit of sending cards every day. She explains that this activity puts her in the "send out to give" spirit, and it affects the things she notices and the deeds she performs every day. Tammy recently attended one of our seminars where she heard my story about my father's money clip. My dad always carried several hundred dollars in a money clip so he could perform random acts of kindness to people in need. This inspired me to carry a money clip with $1,000 in it so I could do the same thing.

On Thanksgiving morning Tammy ran to the grocery store to pick up some last-minute items for her holiday meal. She noticed a lady with three small children walking down the aisle in the store. The lady had been crying. In her "send out to give" spirit Tammy walked up to the lady and asked if she was OK. The lady tearfully explained that she only had $6 to her name and was trying to figure out how to prepare a Thanksgiving meal for her children. Tammy remembered the money-clip story and had a prompting to act. She opened her purse and pulled out all of her cash. She had around $70. She gave the entire amount to this lady in need and wished her and her children the best on this day of Thanksgiving. As Tammy left the grocery store empty handed, she realized this was the best Thanksgiving Day she had ever had.

Tammy is an active participant in the crusade to send out the positives to world. The result is a manifestation of positive experiences that come back to Tammy. I hope the words on these pages will inspire you to always send out your very best to others. It is also my hope that you will help others do the same.

We all have goals to accomplish. We all have dreams to live. We all have a destiny to pursue. There are things in this world that only we can do. There are people in our lives that only we can touch or help at certain times. We must learn to manifest and receive the noble desires of our heart so we can share who we really are with the world.

The best way to do that is to participate in a daily activity that puts you into that vibrational energy of giving. This is a place of "feel good," a place where nourishment to the soul takes place. In this book we have discussed the infinite pathway of energy. This is the pathway that travels around your inner promptings, who you are, and your outer promptings, what you do with who you are. It doesn't matter where you begin as long as you stay focused on both.

When a prompting comes, act. If it is an outer prompting telling you to thank someone, thank them. As you are thanking them, focus on the words you use or the actions you take. Realize that when you have reached into who you are, the inner promptings allow you to act on the outer promptings.

Recognize your own genius. Celebrate it; feel good about it. Know that you are an amazing human being. This creates constant nourishment to your inner and outer promptings. It keeps you in the "feel-good" state and guides you to your genius. This is not difficult. In fact, it is quite easy and it will bring a lifestyle of abundance to you.

The challenge with things being easy to do is that they are also easy not to do. If you get in the habit of sending heartfelt greeting cards and gifts to people every day, recognize the kindness that you offer, celebrate and feel good about it, you will begin to attract and manifest your desires in your life.

Better yet, if you will take the energy generated from this activity and wrap it around your inner promptings, you will take charge and control the manifestation of your desires. How do you do this? Study the first several chapters of this book. Create the stories you desire in your mind; discover the old, unwanted tennis balls (limiting thoughts and beliefs) and drop them. The best way to do this is create the new tennis balls (your positive "I am" statements) and continually send them to yourself or your subconscious mind.

What you send out is what you get back, so send out exactly what you desire to yourself. Celebrate the lives of everyone around you, and your own life will be celebrated.

Always be doing things that put you into a state of "feel good."

CREATE YOUR OWN MAGICAL WONDERLAND

I took my family to Disneyland a few years before this writing. This is the Magic Kingdom, a place where all your dreams come true. On this particular trip Disney was celebrating its fifty-year anniversary. The park has a spectacular fireworks show, and the theme song of the show is the famous Disney song I grew up with. Its lyrics convey a message we should be reminded of often:

When you wish upon a star
Makes no difference who you are
Anything your heart desires will come to you.

Walt Disney lived by this motto and created a magical wonderland for millions to enjoy. His story is truly remarkable. He was a successful icon whose life we should study. He lived simple principles and believed in the power of a dream. He was consistent in his efforts. He focused on his big picture, and the rest is history.

We too can create our own magical wonderland. We too can create a place in our own lives where all our dreams come true. We too can wish upon a star and have anything our heart desires. There are simple principles that will help us manifest our desires and dreams into our lives. As an example, you can identify your desires, write them in present tense ("I am"), and read them or state them numerous times a day.

You need a continuous source of energy to nourish this personal movement in your life. Send an unexpected card with a word of encouragement, a birthday card that shows you cared enough to not forget, or a thank-you card that shares appreciation. These cards will do wonders for the people you send them to, but they will do more for you, the sender. This activity immediately triggers positive energy and begins to attract positive things back to you. When positive things happen, you begin to explore your imagination; you start dreaming again, and you start believing there really is more out there for you. Life is meant to be joyous. We were built for success.

SendOutCards delivers solutions that help you treat people in your life right. As you begin treating people right, you naturally transform into a more positive state of mind. With a daily trigger of sending out cards, you create a positive mindset and become more in tune with treating yourself right. It helps you to treat yourself and others the right way every day.

If we learn to treat ourselves right, we will become better at treating others right. Our system has become one of the greatest personal development tools available in the world today. Why? Because sending out cards triggers positive energy. It is a tool that makes it simple and convenient to live the Golden Rule in your life.

ALWAYS BE AWARE OF WHAT YOU ARE SENDING

We believe in flushing out the negatives and replacing them with positives. Our SendOutCards system delivers those positives, and what we send out comes back to us tenfold in our lives.

I would like to share just a few of the flushing-out principles we discuss in our seminars. This will help you understand how we replace negatives with positives and exponentially expand the positives by sending them out to the world.

You deserve exactly what you send out, and everything you send out is done through thoughts, feelings, words, and deeds.

Focus on the things you want, not on the things you don't want

The things you want make you feel good. The things you don't want make you feel bad. Think about your desires, feel good about them, put them into words ("I am" statements), and go to work on them.

Focus on the language you use when you are reaching out to others

He or she is strange replaced with *He or she is interesting*

I don't like that person (replaced with) *They see things differently than I do.*

I don't agree with your lifestyle replaced with *Hey, I love you anyway.*

You should see things as I do replaced with *It's OK to disagree.*

They don't live my religion replaced with *I respect your beliefs.*

They irritate me replaced with *What if I knew they would be dead in 10 minutes?*

Remember the lyrics in the "Send to Give" song: "Never putting you beneath or above—you and I, other people, we're all equal in love."

Adjusting your thoughts and your language about money

I need money to pay the bills replaced with *The bills are being paid.*

How will I pay the mortgage replaced with *I sure enjoy my new home.*

How can I make more money replaced with *I'm helping people and adding value.*

We need more funds replaced with *The funds are flowing in.*

How do I get out of debt replaced with *My debts are being paid off.*

We sure need a new car replaced with *I love the smell of my new leather seats.*

I will never afford that replaced with *It's nice having the things I want.*

I was not meant for wealth replaced with *I enjoy what my wealth allows me to do.*

I can't afford it replaced with *I choose not to spend my money on that at this time.*

Recognize the use of the words "I am" in your everyday language

We have learned how to use "I am" statements. We must also learn how not to use them. Unfortunately, because we take in so much negativity, we naturally use "I am" statements in a negative way, and many times we don't even know we are doing it. What you send out is what you get back, so you need to be aware of what you are sending out.

I am not feeling well replaced with *I will be better soon.*

I am out of shape replaced with *I am getting more in shape every day.*

I am too tired replaced with *It's time for me to rest.*

I am upset replaced with *I have calmed down.*

I don't get it replaced with *I am figuring this out.*

The list goes on and on. Just two weeks before this writing I was riding ATVs on the motocross track with my sixteen-year-old son and twenty-four-year-old son-in-law. Many people would call this a young man's sport. I took three aggressive laps on the track and pulled over to rest. Some guys about my age were also resting on the side of the track, and I pulled up to them and said, "Man, it's too bad we have to get old, isn't it?" They laughed, and I immediately realized I sent the wrong message to myself. You would be amazed how often even us positive thinkers will catch ourselves using the wrong "I am" language. By being aware of it, we can quickly shift that language so we are always sending the positives we need to.

THE FLUSHING PROCESS

You can see how the flushing process works. The more we align our thoughts, feelings, words, and deeds with the positive, the more positive we will send out to others. By sending those positives out, we attract tenfold those positives in our life. This is a magical process. It works. People not only crave feeling appreciated, they also crave the feeling of hope. People living in a negative world lose hope; it is our job to give that back to them. If we are saying the right things to ourselves, adjusting our language, and staying in that "feel-good" state, we will be the ones delivering that hope to millions of people living in a troubled world. A simple unexpected card filled with appreciation and hope will turn a life around. The sender of that card will actually benefit the most. It is a universal law, and it works whether you believe in it or not.

IT'S HOW YOU MAKE THEM FEEL

Famous author and poet Maya Angelou has written these powerful words: "I've learned that people will forget what you said, people will forget what you did, but people will never forget how you made them feel."

This applies to what you send to others and what you send to yourself. As Lynn Grabhorn said, "It's the feelings that create the energy we send out." The conscious mind thinks; the subconscious mind feels. That is why feelings are the most powerful way to receive energy.

Who better than Helen Keller to teach us this? She said, "The best and most beautiful things in the world cannot be seen or even touched. They must be felt with the heart."

WRITE IT DOWN!

Jim Rohn is one of my favorite speakers. He is well known for his three-word phrase "Write it down," and he is best known for his lifelong counsel to keep a journal. In fact, he, along with numerous motivational experts, believes whatever you write or type will manifest itself in your life exactly as you write it. This is why "I am" statements are so effective. I believe it is also why greeting cards are so effective. Think about it: By writing words of encouragement and celebration in a greeting card, we send a subtle, "feel-good" message to our subconscious. Whether the feeling is a celebration of our lives or the lives of others doesn't matter. It is a message that is written down.

As Rohn would say, it is also why journals are so effective. Our minds are going a million miles an hour. The subconscious is throwing ideas into the conscious so quickly that we need ways to capture those thoughts as they come to us. Rohn has spent a lifetime writing his journals. He will tell you they are his most prized possessions and he cites them as the reason for his massive success.

JOURNAL YOUR WAY TO SUCCESS

The simple act of writing things down will take you better than halfway toward your goal. I want you to think about the significance of that. *Write it down, write it down, write it down.*

Write down your goals, your dreams, your desires, your stories, your thoughts. Anything that makes you stop and think should be written down. So how do you keep all this organized, and where do you write it?

The best way to keep a journal is in a three-ring binder with lined paper and organizer tabs. Obviously those tabs will create sections in your journal where you can file entries in the right places. You also want to be able to open your journal and find a blank page to write on. I always leave about twenty blank pages in the opening section of my journal. This allows me to just start writing. Whatever *prompting* you have, you can simply start writing it down. Don't worry about where it's going to go; just write. When you are finished, you can place it wherever it needs to go in your journal.

Your sections are up to you. A journal is a personal thing, and it will become your most prized possession if you build it right. You decide how to categorize your entries.

Here is a list of the categories I have in my journal:
1. Purpose
2. "I am" statements (present-tense goals and the "whys" behind those goals)
3. Thoughts/quotes
4. Ideas
5. Articles of inspiration and lists of books to read
6. Lessons/speeches (outlines of speeches, training sessions, and lessons)
7. Gratitude (list the things I am thankful for)
8. Journal entries (my collection of stories)

Many of the thoughts and stories you are reading in this book have come straight out of my journals. I am amazed when I go back and read thoughts and entries from years past.

You will notice the first four categories in my journal are essentially stories in my mind; they are my inner promptings, or who I am. Categories Five and Six are actions that nourish my inner promptings. Categories Seven and Eight are stories of my life. They are my outer promptings, or what I am doing with who I am.

What you send out is what you get back. A journal is a way for you to capture your inner promptings and send them out to yourself. It is also a way for you to collect your life stories so you have them to share with others.

THE POWER OF THE JOURNAL

Our family recently moved into our new dream home. When we were unpacking, I pulled out one of my journals. I took a moment to browse through the sections. The "I am" section had a list of statements that, when written, were stories in my mind. As I walked from room to room and from the home to the garages, I was looking at the manifestation of everything I had written in that journal. It was an amazing experience. I had described the vehicles, the toys, the garages, the den, the library, the wood floors, the kitchen, and on and on.

I guess I owe this one to Rohn. I took his advice and kept journals, and I have to say I would agree with him: I attribute much of where I am today to the journals.

WRAPPING THIS UP

While reading my journal, I came across this story I wrote down about four years prior to this writing. Here is the entry:

I have two sons, Bo and Sawyer. They think they are really tough. We were wrestling on my bed the other night. I told them I would give them $100 if they could get me off the bed. I gave them ten minutes to do it. They tried and tried and tried. They learned that Papa Bear (that would be me) is still the king of my household. It got to where they only had one minute left. They were getting desperate. Their mother came to their rescue in the final seconds. They wrapped me in the blanket on the bed, and the three of them pulled until the blanket, with me in it, crashed to the floor. With their mother's help they were able to get the job done.

There is a lesson or a message in every story that happens to us. After writing this story in my journal I added the following thoughts:

The way to move and inspire yourself and others to greatness is to wrap yourself and others up with kindness. Gladly receive the help of loved ones and have lots of fun along the way.

What a great way to wrap up this chapter. What you send out is what you get back. As Tony Robbins says: "Life will give you anything you ask of it." Be kind to yourself, be kind to others, and enjoy the greatness that will come back to you.

"To one who has faith, no explanation is necessary. To one without faith, no explanation is possible."

SAINT THOMAS AQUINAS

"Our belief at the beginning of a doubtful undertaking is the one thing that inspires the successful outcome of your venture."

WILLIAM JAMES

"If you are not living by faith then you will automatically be living by fear."

ROBERT SCHULLER

CHAPTER 11

Do You Believe?

We have shared some wonderful stories and discussed some amazing philosophies in this book. They work if you are a believer. One of my "I am" statements says, "I am a believer." I have found it is much better to focus on what you believe in rather than what you don't believe in. Belief creates possibility, renders hope, and delivers an abundance of energy. Non-belief creates doubt, renders negativity, and delivers a depletion of energy.

Along with this it is important to be *pro* something rather than *anti* anything. Being for something keeps you in the positive state of belief. Being against something keeps you in the negative state of non-belief. Now the last thing I want to do here is get political. I believe we all have a right to believe in and support anything we want as long as it does not cause harm to others.

My suggestion is that we stay on the positive side of what we support, rather than on the negative side of what we don't support. Be a believer and stand strong on the positive side of what you have a passion for. The best way to do this is to keep yourself in the spirit of believing.

In the "thoughts" category of my journal I have a list of things I believe in. I encourage you to write your own list. This is one of the most powerful ways to tap your inner promptings. Your beliefs represent who you are.

Here is my list:

I am a believer

I believe there is a lot more good in the world than bad

I believe you can do anything you set your mind to

I believe we are all created equal, yet we are all unique

I believe everyone has something only he or she can contribute to the world

I believe love and gratitude are the two greatest forces in the universe

I believe you deserve and you will receive exactly what you send out

I believe written expressions create an energy that makes our world a better place

I believe a picture is worth a thousand words

I believe a prompting is a gift that must be acted upon

I believe life is an adventure and should be lived with passion

I believe in a person's right to follow his or her heart, and those that do show great courage

I believe in respecting another's right to believe as they choose

I believe faith and love will deliver a life of abundance

I believe we are changing the world one card at a time

I believe in living "happily ever after"

I believe friendship is what life is all about

I believe my friends are the best people in the world

I believe crystals in freshly fallen snow are the most
  beautiful sight in the world
I believe an ocean beach is a magical place where you
  can dream and feel at peace
I believe life is a collection of stories
I believe wealth is available in abundance
I believe every year will be a year of wonderful stories
  and abundant prosperity
I believe in Santa Claus. No, seriously, I really believe in
  Santa Claus
I believe miracles come from the goodness of people's
  hearts
I believe in Jesus Christ, and I cherish the annual
  celebration of his birth
I believe it is OK to tell you what I believe because I
  respect you for what you believe
I believe all mankind has a desire to love and be loved,
  and that is all we really need to know

I believe we can all reflect on the power of believing. It's important to believe in good things, to know our world is filled with hope and that we can make a difference and bring good tidings of great joy. I believe that prayers are answered, especially when people choose to be an answer to others' prayers.

A LITTLE GIRL WHO BELIEVED

My father tells a story from the days when I was very young. Our family would travel to the mountains and cut down our Christmas tree every year. On one of these occasions we found the perfect Christmas tree, cut it down, strapped it to the top of the family car, and drove home. When we returned, we got out of the car only to find that the tree was no longer on top of the car. Somewhere on the way our perfect tree had fallen from the car. My father decided to drive back down the road to see if he could find it.

About four miles away he noticed a spot in the road where it looked as if a tree had fallen. He also noticed that someone had dragged the tree from the road, up a sidewalk, and into a home at the side of the road.

My dad walked up and knocked on the door. A young and excited girl answered. My dad asked if her parents were home.

She said, "Yes, but they are busy." Then, in her excitement, she said, "And guess what just happened?"

With surprise my dad asked, "What?"

"Our family knelt down and said a prayer asking God to bring us a Christmas tree," she said. "My daddy lost his job so we could not afford to buy one this year. When we finished our prayer, I got up and looked out our front window, and there was a beautiful Christmas tree lying at our front curb." With tears in her eyes the little girl said, "Now we can have a wonderful Christmas."

With tears in his eyes my father said, "Merry Christmas," returned to his car, and drove home.

You see, miracles do happen. Prayers are answered. Santa is real. Goodness is in abundant supply. The little girl in this story had amazing faith. She truly believed God would deliver her family a Christmas tree, and look what happened.

❖

All great things in life begin as a concept, a belief in a new possibility. To manifest greatness we must begin with faith. Faith is the ability to see things as real before they are manifested. The New Testament tells us, "Faith is the substance of things hoped for and the evidence of things not seen."

We mentioned earlier that the power of the "I am" is that you already are. Those who understand this believe they already are the things they have written in their "I am" statements. This is faith at its finest. This is the ability to see things as real before others might see them as real. This is a substance of things hoped for, and it is where greatness begins.

CONCEIVE IT, BELIEVE IT, ACHIEVE IT

Napoleon Hill, in his classic book *Think and Grow Rich,* explains, "What the mind of man can conceive and believe it can achieve."

He also mentions, "Faith is the starting point for all accumulations. Faith is the basis of all miracles and all mysteries which cannot be analyzed by the rules of science—faith is the only known antidote for failure."

Those are powerful words from one of the greatest personal development instructors in history.

> *If you believe in greatness, then you will attract greatness.*
> *If you believe in abundance, then you will attract abundance.*
> *If you believe there is far more good in the world than bad, then you will attract that which is good in your life.*

I challenge you to believe in greatness. Write your list of positive beliefs. Add to that list whenever a new thought comes to you. This will put you in the positive mindset of believing. This is where greatness happens.

❋

In the documentary film *What the BLEEP Do We Know?,* there were many concepts shared about belief patterns and how they shape our lives. A friend of mine recommended that I see this film and take notes. Being the journal guy that I am, I brought my journal and my favorite pen to the movie with me.

Here are some of the notes I wrote:

"We only see what we believe is possible. What we believe is possible is based on our conditioning. Our conditioning creates our beliefs about ourselves and others. We do not see ourselves, others, or the world with our eyes. We literally see what we believe we see. We see what we tell ourselves."

I watched this documentary with my wife Jodi. There was a scene in the film where a woman, about thirty-five years old, stood in front of a mirror in her underwear. She was in decent shape and appeared to be, perhaps, ten to fifteen pounds over her ideal weight. She looked good. What the audience was seeing was the woman I just described. The image in the mirror is what she was seeing. That image looked totally different. The image she was seeing was a woman about forty to fifty pounds overweight with extra shape around the hips and lower torso area of her body.

I looked over at Jodi and said, "There is no way that lady sees that big of a difference." Jodi looked at me with tears in her eyes and said, "I live that every day." I was blown away. I could not believe it.

Here is my wife, a gorgeous size six, in the best shape of her life, still seeing herself far more out of shape than others see her. When Jodi was in junior high school, someone commented that she was fat. That ridiculous comment stuck with her for more than twenty-five years. It conditioned her mind to believe she was overweight. As a result, this is the way she saw herself.

In the same film Dr. Joseph Dispenza shared the concept that because our beliefs are what we see, we can create any reality we desire. With this knowledge he wakes up in the morning and consciously creates his day the way he wants it to happen. This is a powerful concept. Many call this segment intending. This is where you visualize your day or an activity in your day the way you would like to see it happen. You state in present tense the way you see the experience happening.

What you are doing is conditioning your mind to believe that a reality you desire is happening. Most of the time we allow pre-conditioning to determine a reality we don't desire. Talk about the power of what we believe in.

From these lessons I have learned that I can create the realities I desire simply by believing what I choose has already happened. As an example, before every seminar I teach, speech I give, or lesson I conduct, I do the following: I look over the list of people who will be in attendance at the event. I make myself consciously aware that I am not there for me; I am there for them. In other words, the upcoming event is not so much about how well I perform as it is how well I can connect with the people there. I make the event about the people in the seats and not about me.

I then will say a silent prayer and thank God for the amazing day we shared together. I will thank him for the incredible energy felt, the interaction enjoyed, and the connections made. You will notice I am treating all these things as if they had already happened. Sometimes I will even write my desired outcome on an index card and read it a few times before I go on stage.

Say what you want about this idea. All I can tell you is I have seen amazing results from doing it. In my personal life I have further evidence of how powerful this concept works.

❖

I have always said prayers. For many years of my life my prayers consisted of thanking God for things and asking him for things. For the past five years I have simply given prayers of thanksgiving, thanking God for all my blessings—past, present, and future. I believe in a God who is waiting to shower his blessings of abundance upon us. We get in his way with our limiting beliefs. Many people are faithful in saying their prayers but block the blessings with the thoughts and words they use—things like, "It would be nice if," "I really need this," or "I don't have that, so what am I to do?" kind of language.

Instead of getting in our own way and even in God's way, may I suggest that we simplify the process. Simply pray words of thanksgiving. I believe in a loving heavenly father as my source, and I use prayer to communicate with him. Whomever or whatever your source is, communicate in the spirit of thanksgiving and watch what happens.

SPEAKING OF BELIEFS

I believe I am in control of my destiny
I believe I can do all things through Christ who
*   strengthens me*
I believe it's OK to tell you that because I respect
*   whatever positive source you have*
I believe we are all destined for greatness

I believe we will be challenged, we will be tested, and we
will prevail triumphant
I believe in a life of abundance and that all things are
meant to come together for our good
I believe in people
I believe in me
I believe our purpose is to love and be loved and that our
biggest test is in how we break down our difference
with others
I believe we are our greatest asset or our biggest liability,
and I choose to be an asset in my own life and in the
lives of others
I believe it is time for people to take charge of their lives
I believe it is time to dust off your dreams and make
them happen
I believe every day is an amazing day
I believe the sun is always shining, even when storms
have set in
I believe that in the darkest moments the stars appear

As my good friend Super Dave says, it's time to "find clarity of purpose and wake up to abundance." It's time to believe in your purpose and know you are the best you in the history of the world.

Conceive it, believe it, and make it happen in your life.

"It has been my experience that folks who have no vices have very few virtues."

ABRAHAM LINCOLN

CHAPTER 12

Loosen the Grip

I grew up riding motorcycles. I am still riding motorcycles, so I guess that means I am still growing up. I learned that, when riding motorcycles, if you have a tight grip on the handlebars, your wrists and arms get tired really fast.

You really notice this when you race motorcycles because you are riding hard and fast while trying to stay ahead of the next rider. Your mind and body tense up with the pressure of competition. Because of this, inexperienced motorcycle racers will tighten their grip on the handlebars and experience fatigue much more quickly than when they are just riding for fun. As soon as a rider consciously loosens the grip on the handlebars, he begins to ride smoother and with less effort. As a result, he actually goes faster.

Our family rides anything with handlebars, so we are all familiar with loosening the grip. Whenever any of us start complaining or arguing, someone will say, "Loosen the grip." Whenever any of us worry about the past or stress about something in the future, someone will say, "Loosen the grip." Whenever any of us meddle in someone else's business or complain about a circumstance, someone will say, "Loosen the grip."

This has become a valuable tool in our home. It helps us run our lives more smoothly and with less fatigue. When things are smooth and calm, you find yourself in vibrational harmony with who you really are. You are in a "feel-good" state where desires and goals can be manifested more quickly. Remember, when you loosen the grip, you ride smoother and go faster to your destination.

Another lesson I learned from racing motorcycles was the more I focused on the other riders, the sloppier I would ride. Experienced racers learn that when they focus on their own race, they ride better. If I choose my line on the track, loosen the grip, and race my race, I finish better every time. I have also learned I can apply these lessons to everything I set out to accomplish in my life.

Activities such as sending greeting cards provide you with a daily mechanism that will help you loosen the grip in your life. After sending an unexpected card, you are naturally in a state of "feel good." You are calm. Your heart, mind, and emotions are in alignment. This is where amazing things start to happen because you are in vibrational harmony.

You can carry this harmony into a manifestation of successful living. Past failures or disappointments are gone forever; future expectations and desires are on their way. It doesn't matter what other people are saying, thinking, or doing in their lives—it only matters what you say, think, and do in yours. In other words, loosen the grip.

Many of you are involved in various ventures because you want to build a successful business that provides you with residual income. You see those ventures as a way to realize the big dreams you've had since you were a kid. You can easily do this if you loosen the grip. It doesn't matter what has happened in the past, and it doesn't matter what other people are saying, thinking, or doing. It only matters that you stay consistent with your race. Find your daily process of action and be consistent with it.

That's all there is to it. Loosen the grip, choose your line, race your race, and have fun. Success will follow.

I recall a time when my two boys and I went to the motocross track in Delta, Utah. We rented a motor home and spent spring-break weekend at the track. We had a great time. We got there on a Thursday evening, and the boys were anxious to get out there and ride. I needed to make a conference call, so I sent them on the track and watched as I conducted my call. The motor home was parked at the top of a hill, and you could look down and see all the action.

During the conference call we were discussing the importance of consistency. As business associates we had defined a simple process of action for building our business. We had predetermined that there were eight basic things an individual needed to do every day. We called it the "Daily 8." The most important element to making the Daily 8 work was consistent action. With consistent action individuals could get really good at building their businesses.

While we were having this discussion, I was watching my two sons on the track. This was a new track for them, and they had to get used to it. I noticed with each lap they grew consistently smoother and faster. The more familiar they got, the more confident they became. The first few laps they were slowly rolling over the jumps. By the time my conference call ended they were catching major air and clearing every jump. They found their line, loosened the grip, and enjoyed the ride.

Whatever venture, project, career, or life pursuit you are involved with, I suggest you learn the daily process that will help you succeed. Keep track of what you are doing, stay consistent, and loosen the grip. I would also suggest that your simple, everyday life will be enhanced if you relax more, worry less, and find the good in every moment.

I recently studied two books that really helped me with this concept. The first one was *The Power of Now* by Eckhart Tolle; the second was *Loving What Is* by Byron Katie.

The Power of Now teaches the importance of living in the now. Most people spend their time focusing on the past or worrying about the future. The problem with this is the only thing we have is *now*. Life is lived in the *now*. If we are focused on the past or future, then we cannot enjoy what's going on at the moment. When I realized I had done this a lot in the past, I vowed to focus on living in the present. It has brought a greater joy and peace to my life. I learned there are many perfect moments in the *now*. A great way to relax and loosen the grip in my life is to stay *present*.

Loving What Is teaches there are three kinds of business: 1) Your business, 2) other people's business, and 3) God's business. The challenge here is that most people spend their time in other people's business or in God's business and less time in the one area that they control: their own business.

Think about it. When we analyze the gossip, the negative discussions, and the worry conversations in our life, we are either in someone else's business or God's business, and there is nothing we can do to change any of that. So why do people spend so much time there? By simply realizing this tendency, you can shift your focus to your own business where you do have control. Again, this helps you relax, loosen the grip, and live a better quality of life.

For us to be in a state of "feel good," we need to *relax*. Living in the *now* and focusing on our own business is a great way to do that. Having a project with an action plan is also a great way to stay engaged in building and growing.

FINDING YOUR MARGARITAVILLE

Several years ago I was a guest on a yacht that traveled up the Ohio River out of Louisville, Kentucky. Some friends and business associates and I were out to have a good time on a Friday afternoon. As we made our way out of the harbor, the captain turned on the stereo and began playing Jimmy Buffett's greatest hits. This was the first time I had a connection with Jimmy's music. He really has a way of helping you get into the "feel good" of the moment. The boat ride was an adventure, and Jimmy's music made it a memorable event.

Since that experience I have been a big fan of Jimmy Buffett. I recently learned that he not only composes feel-good music, but he also writes adventurous feel-good novels. Jimmy is known for his connection with sandy beaches and open seas. For years he lived in Key West, Florida, where he composed music, performed at local bars, and became known as a good old local boy out for a good time. Another long-standing resident of Key West was a guy by the name of Ernest Hemingway. He was, of course, a world-famous novelist whom many consider the greatest writer ever to come out of America.

Jimmy Buffett has mentioned that Hemingway inspired him to pursue a second career as a writer. Jimmy is an example of someone who lives his dreams. He has made it to the top in two professions, producing inspiring works in song and the written word. Of all the people I look up to, Jimmy is the best at teaching the importance of being in a state of "feel good." He does this in his songs, he writes about it in his books, but most importantly, he lives it in his life. I don't know Jimmy personally, but I can bet that the primary reason he has achieved massive success in his life is because he has followed his own heart, pursued his dreams and stayed in the "feel good" along the way.

One of his most famous songs is titled "Margaritaville." He has written a book titled *Tales from Margaritaville*. When you first listen to his song and read this book, Margaritaville seems to be a destination—a place somewhere in the Caribbean with sandy beaches, clear blue waters, palm trees, good music, and lots of fun. You soon find out, however, that Margaritaville is a state of mind. Margaritaville is anywhere you want it to be.

The message Jimmy gives the world is a simple one: Life is an adventure—something to be enjoyed. We need to find our own Margaritaville to become who we were meant to be. We have mentioned that being in a state of "feel good" is crucial to your success. This is where you generate positive energy and send that energy into the world. In doing so, you attract what you send out, and more good comes to you.

If you want healthy relationships, a wealthy lifestyle, and a happy life, simply find your Margaritaville. Get into the state of "feel good" every day. Focus on your big-picture life, and don't let the little-picture stuff get in your way. Start your day by sending an unexpected card to a friend, a family member, or a client. Express your appreciation for that person. Consistency is the key. If you will do this every day, universal law will guarantee a state of "feel good" in your life.

If you act on your promptings consistently, you will be guided to your genius within. You will also create a network of people along the way that will be committed to your success. Why? Because people crave feeling appreciated. If you act on your promptings and help people feel appreciated, they will naturally be committed and loyal to you.

FINDING MARGARITAVILLE IN HAWAII

A few years back, we conducted a seminar in Honolulu, Hawaii. What an incredible visit to the Hawaiian Islands. The seminar was spectacular. The spirit of "aloha" was really fun. The hospitality we received was amazing. Numerous people from Hawaii made sure our stay was an enjoyable one. We were invited on radio shows, we were treated to a Saturday night show on Waikiki Beach, and we were taken on a memorable sailboat ride along the beach front of Waikiki. Gifts were delivered to our hotel room. We are deeply grateful for the kindness shown to us. Life is truly a collection of stories, and we collected many on this memorable trip.

I mentioned that we went on a sailboat ride. It was an overcast evening with windy weather and large water swells to sail through. Fourteen people were on board, with twelve of us from the SendOut-Cards family. It was a magical evening. Great company, fun times, and breathtaking views. About one hour into our voyage the captain spotted some dolphins. Before we knew it, we had a school of dolphins swimming and playing along the front of our small vessel. They were so close we could reach over the side of the boat and touch them. Our captain, who loves dolphins, had never seen them swim along a small vessel like that. He had been sailing for twenty-two years.

Our group took many pictures, and many cards containing those photos were sent. We had enjoyed a moment in Margaritaville and were able to capture that moment and share it through pictures and the written word. This is an incredible way to live.

I ended up with a picture of me on the bow of the boat looking back at everyone. I had on Hawaiian shorts, sunglasses, and puka shells. I was hanging on to the railing with one hand and showing a big thumbs-up with the other hand. Every time I see that picture, I'm instantly taken back to that moment when I was in a state of "feel good."

I took that picture and loaded it on a PicturePlus greeting card. I wrote my list of "I am" statements inside the card and sent the card to myself in the mail. This is one of the most powerful personal-development activities I have ever done. By looking at the card I instantly feel the emotions of that "feel-good" state. With those emotions I open the card and read my "I am" statements. This is a celebration of who I am.

There are many ways to create that 'feel-good" emotion, making it possible to loosen the grip. You can listen to inspiring music or motivational messages, attend inspirational events, meditate, read, or send and receive greeting cards.

I recall an experience that took place with our dear friends Dave and Lori Smith. Lori had been recently diagnosed with a large aneurysm in her brain. She had open-brain surgery where doctors went in and clamped off the aneurysm. This is a delicate and serious surgery, and it had us all very concerned. The operation took several hours, and we were all sitting in the intensive care unit's waiting room. As family and friends waited in that room, things grew tense. Worry and doubt set in for many. Then the miracle happened. To relieve some of his own stress, Dave pulled a stack of greeting cards from his bag. He had over 100 cards that had been sent to wish Lori well during surgery. He began to look at each one and then pass them on to the next person.

The mood and energy of that room instantly shifted. Instead of frowns of concern, there were smiles of joy. Instead of feelings of doubt, there was confidence and peace. Everyone in the waiting room took notice. Even those who were not part of our group caught on to the "feel good" those cards carried. It was truly an amazing experience none of us will ever forget.

There is true magic in greeting cards. It is not the card itself; it's the message on the card. It is pure energy, the positive kind—the energy that changes lives and makes the world a better place.

As this was going on in the waiting room, Lori was down the hall on the operating table going through the biggest challenge of her life. I truly believe Lori felt that energy as well. The doctors later told us that her operation ran smoother than any they had previously performed. During an operation like this, the patient's vital signs normally go up and down during the surgery, and half the surgeon's battle is keeping the vital signs where they need to be. In Lori's surgery her vitals never varied. The doctors mentioned that Lori was calm and confident, a valiant fighter who made things simple for the doctors.

The stack of greeting cards helped us "loosen the grip" in the waiting room. The unexpected greeting card you send every day will help you "loosen the grip" on the crazy things that appear to be going on in your life. Staying focused on your own race, your own desires, your own "I am" statements, and your own daily actions will help you "loosen the grip" and enjoy the ride.

FINAL THOUGHT

The objective of this book is to explain the power of the inner and outer promptings, introduce the philosophy of how they guide your life, and suggest ideas on how you can free yourself to feel them. By loosening the grip, you can calm the clutter of your conscious mind so that you recognize the workings of your subconscious, where your promptings are born.

The calming effect will prepare you for the principles of abundance that we will discuss next.

"He knows not his own strength that hath

not met adversity."

BEN JONSON

"Your net worth to the world is usually determined by what remains after your bad habits are subtracted from your good ones."

BENJAMIN FRANKLIN

"The secret of success is making your vocation your vacation."

MARK TWAIN

"Rich people constantly learn and grow. Poor people think they already know."

T. HARV EKER

CHAPTER 13

Wealth in Abundance

In this chapter I am going to talk about *money*! How does that make you feel? What is your first impression after reading that sentence? Studies have shown the word "money" is one of the top five words in the English language to spark a negative emotion. The main reason for this is that most people don't have enough of it.

Other reasons include our preconditioned beliefs about money and the judgments we place on money. In this chapter I will talk a lot about money and even the things money can buy. The examples we give may seem materialistic to some but exciting to others. You will also read how money allows you to give back, to support others, and to create positive change in the world.

Most importantly we will discuss how financial abundance brings your promptings into focus and allows you to act on those promptings in life-changing ways. Today you might act on a prompting by sending a greeting card to someone. A few years from now you may start a foundation as a result of acting on a prompting.

Imagine hearing that a loved one living 3,000 miles away is in need. You are prompted to jump on a plane and fly to their hometown and surprise them with your support. You need the money and the time to be able to act on promptings at that level. I remember when my brother died I had friends from faraway places who made the effort to be at his funeral. Some of those friends didn't even know my brother, but they knew me, and they wanted to show they cared.

Their support had an amazing impact on me. I will never forget those friends for how they made me feel. I vowed that when my friends needed to feel supported, for any reason, I would be in a position where I could be there if prompted to do so. I also vowed that I would be in a financial position to help if financial assistance was needed.

When my brother was killed, my father's business was in a tough position. Money was very tight, and the expenses of an unexpected funeral were daunting. He remembers a lifelong friend, who wishes to remain anonymous, coming to the funeral. As he greeted my father he gave him an envelope and told him to put it in his suit pocket.

With everything going on Dad forgot about the envelope. Later that night while undressing, Dad noticed the envelope. He pulled it out and found enough money in it to pay for the entire funeral expense. That man acted on a prompting and created a loyal friend for life. If you remember, my dad was the one who always carried extra cash in his money clip for the purpose of helping people. Almost every time we ate out as a family, I saw my dad pay for someone else's meal. Now, in a time of need, someone showed up to do it for him. As the saying goes, what you send out is what you get back.

After hearing this story I vowed I would be one of those guys showing up with an envelope. That takes money.

❋

Growing up I had mentors and heroes I looked up to. Fortunately for me, my number one hero was my dad. I have already shared many stories about how Mom and Dad influenced me for good. In addition to Dad, there were other grown-ups in my early life who made a difference for me.

Larry Good lived just a few houses up the street. He was big-time into hunting, fishing, snowmobiling, and boating, and Larry got me interested in snowmobiling. He had a huge garage attached to his house, and we used to work on snowmobiles during the week and then go riding on the weekends. Larry was always there, encouraging us kids to dream big and do what we love. Larry passed away several years ago. At his funeral, I walked up and greeted his wife Joann. She looked at me with a tear in her eye and said, "Kody Bateman, you were always one of Larry's favorites." I will never forget that moment. I'm sure that Larry had many favorites, but to be considered one of them really meant a lot to me.

George Turner also lived in the neighborhood. He was into the boating and camping scene, and he loved being with people. When George was around, there was a story to tell and fun to be had. I remember when I was twelve or thirteen, several kids in the neighborhood loved getting together to play pool. George found out about this and decided to hold a pool tournament in his home. He went out and bought trophies and everything. George was amazing at recognizing people for their accomplishments. By the way, I won that tournament and still have the first-place trophy.

Larry Oreno was a close personal friend with my dad. They did a lot of business together, and Larry and his family would go boating and camping with us. Larry always treated us kids as equals. He was one of the boys—our friend.

Alan Deitline is a guy who came along and married Sandy Hale. Sandy was a close friend to my mother, so Alan and Sandy became friends with Mom and Dad. Alan was larger than life. He was the tall,

John Wayne-cowboy type of guy who commanded your attention. When I was young, Alan and Sandy lived in California and owned a ranch in southern Utah. I remember visiting them in California where they would show us around Hollywood and Glendale. I also remember summer trips in Grover, Utah, where they owned a ranch and my family eventually purchased property. Alan built a beautiful home on a hill in Grover. I was amazed by this home and by the guy who built it. I used to spend hours drawing this home and others like it. As a young boy I was dreaming of building a home like that someday.

I could name many other heroes in my life, but these guys all had something in common: They owned their own businesses, they were adventurous, they had fun, they did what they wanted to, they used their possessions as tools to serve others, and they had money.

WEALTH BEGINS WITH A WHY

In sharing these stories I defined my "why" for creating wealth. I had mentors and heroes who helped me define that "why" as I was growing up. I knew early on that I wanted to be the guy with the envelope. I wanted to be adventurous, have fun, do what I chose to do, own my own business, and use my possessions as tools to serve others.

I also love to collect stories and celebrate life every day. I can do those things with or without money, but I always figured it would be more fun to do it with money. I am an adventurous guy. I like to explore and try new things. I love to travel and meet new people. I love to go fast, and I love anything with a fast motor. I love to play in the water during the summer and on the snow in the winter. I love to do all those things with my family and friends.

I have a passion for personal development. I love to read, write, ponder, pray, and be inspired. My personal-development journey has taught me a great deal about making money. I love what Jim Rohn says: "It's not about the money you acquire in life. It's about the person you become as you acquire it." This really helped me as I began the process of making money. I knew if I became a student of personal development, I would have a greater chance of reaching my potential and enjoying a higher-quality life. The principles I learned would help me in my business ventures and my investments. They would also help me to *be me*. The inner prompting is who I am, and you just read about who I am as a person.

On this journey I have learned several lessons about manifesting an abundance of wealth in my life. Those lessons are simple and easy to follow. They are also easy not to follow. It's your choice. I choose to follow them and live a life of abundance. If you care to follow, read on. Learn it, study it, do it, and teach others to do the same. Here we go.

LESSON #1: THE FOUNDATION OF WEALTH IS IN THE WHY BEHIND THE WHY

I learned a valuable lesson from a young boy named Caleb Mc-Falls. At the time of this writing Caleb is the eight-year-old son of my assistant Leann.

Caleb is the curious type. He likes to know the why behind everything. His younger brother has the same name as I do, so Caleb always calls me by my full name. Recently the McFalls family took a trip with us to Lake Powell and stayed several days with us on our houseboat. Caleb loved to go for rides on the Sea-Doos. Early one morning Caleb came up to me and said, "Kody Bateman, will you take me for a ride on the Sea-Doo?"

I said, "I sure will, but I better top it off with gas first."

"Why?" Caleb asked.

I said, "It's always nice to have the tanks full."

"Why?" Caleb asked.

I said, "I like the tanks to be full so they are ready for the day."

"Why?" Caleb asked.

"Well," I said, "If you start the day with full tanks, everyone can take turns throughout the day without needing to stop and fill them up with gas."

"Oh," he said. "Now that's a great reason."

Did you notice what Caleb did? He kept asking "why?" until he got to the real why. Once he had the real why, he was satisfied. No more questions. We took off and had a great ride on the Sea-Doo.

If you ask the "why" behind your "whys," you can get to the real reason. The initial "whys" are what you think. The real "why" is what you feel.

LESSON #2: FEEL YOUR WHY, AND YOU WILL MANIFEST IT

Let me give you an example:

In Chapter Three I told the story about our dream home. I shared how we created an "I am" statement saying, "We are enjoying our new dream home." We then stated the initial whys behind having this dream home. We mentioned all of the benefits of the home, things like enjoying the garages for the toys, the library for the books, the den for writing and study, the kitchen for gourmet cooking, the game rooms for entertainment, and on and on. We took a picture of the home and made the dream visual. This was a great manifestation exercise, but it wasn't until we got to the real "why" that things really started to happen.

I explained that when my mother passed away, I reflected on how she created a home as a place of refuge. Her home was a place where everyone could come and feel welcome. This was the real "why" behind Jodi and me obtaining this dream home. We wanted a place of refuge where our family and friends could come and feel at home. My mother kept the doors open for the neighborhood to come and enjoy. We wanted the opportunity to do the same thing.

We wrote the original statement and visualized the home in a greeting card we sent to ourselves. We did that three years before we purchased the home. For two of those three years we had not gotten down to the real "why." You know, the one that we could feel. It wasn't until my mother passed away that we discovered the real "why." One year later, through miraculous events and alignments, we moved into that dream home.

Now, had we learned from Caleb's example, we could have done this much more quickly. If we had simply kept asking "why," we would have drilled down to the real "why" behind the home much sooner. Once you define the real "whys" in your life, the stars align to help you live them.

LESSON #3: CREATE A WEALTHY MINDSET

One of my most memorable seminars was at the Marina Del Ray Hotel in Marina Del Ray, California. This hotel is right on the marina. Our hotel room looked over the boat docks where beautiful sailboats and motor yachts rested in their slips. The meeting room where we held the seminar had big windows along the outer wall, and you could look out and see the marina in full view. The scent of the ocean was delivered by a cool breeze, and you could take it all in as you stepped outside the meeting room onto a deck overlooking the water. This was a perfect location for an incredible event.

Southern California is truly an amazing place, a land with sunshine, blue skies, sandy ocean beaches, and a world of abundance all around you. My family came with me to the Marina Del Ray event. We flew into Newport Beach and drove down to the Newport Bay area to have lunch. We pulled into a restaurant with valet parking and a $350,000 Rolls Royce sitting next to other luxury cars and sports cars. I have teenage kids, and their eyes were popping out of their heads. Southern California is truly a land of abundance. You see it in the lifestyles and attitudes of the people you meet there.

At the Marina Del Ray event we did a wealthy-mindset exercise with those in attendance. This is a simple exercise that defines how wealthy people think, feel, and act. We made it through this exercise in record time. Why? Because the people in attendance already had a wealth-building mindset. At other events around the world we spend lots of time discussing these concepts because people don't understand them. Not in So-Cal. This is truly a land of abundance. Is it coincidence that you see so much prosperity there and the people who reside there have a mindset for building wealth? I don't think so. This was a refreshing experience. This is a place where I like to hang out. Abundant thinking is contagious, and I want to be around it as much as I can.

What does a wealthy mindset look like?

Wealthy people focus on their big picture or purpose. Poor people focus on their little pictures or daily routines.

Wealthy people focus on the long-term gain from their efforts. Poor people focus on their short-term results.

Wealthy people have a mindset for abundance. Poor people have a mindset for security or control.

Wealthy people go outside of their comfort zones. Poor people do all they can to protect their comfort zones.

Wealthy people see the glass as half full. Poor people see the glass as half empty.

Wealthy people never play the game of "victim." Poor people become a "victim" in most of their dealings.

One of the most powerful quotes I have read to date comes from T. Harv Eker, who says, "It's time to decide: You can be a victim or you can be rich, but you can't be both." He goes on to say, "There is no such thing as a really rich victim." I highly recommend his book *Secrets of the Millionaire Mind.*

Wealthy people choose both. Poor people choose either/or.

Wealthy people learn and grow. Poor people think they know.

Wealthy people focus on their why. Poor people focus on their how.

Wealthy people spend time on foundational training. Poor people skip to how-to training.

Wealthy people visualize what they desire. Poor people wonder how they will ever get what they desire.

Wealthy people send out abundance with their thoughts, feelings, words, and deeds. Poor people send out scarcity with their thoughts, feelings, words, and deeds.

Wealthy people leverage their time, talents, and money with people. Poor people guard their time, talents, and money with fear.

Wealthy people don't think about it; they do it. Poor people think about it and don't do it.

Wealthy people celebrate the success of others. Poor people judge the success of others.

Wealthy people believe they can have their cake and eat it too. Poor people don't believe they deserve cake, so they order a doughnut, focus on the hole, and wonder why they have nothing.

Wealthy people know how to set their money blueprint. Poor people don't know they have a money blueprint.

LESSON #4: TAKE CONTROL OF YOUR MONEY BLUEPRINT

Eker teaches us about money blueprints. Again, I highly recommend you study his work. We all have a blueprint in our minds of how much we are worth or how much money we can expect to make. We make whatever that blueprint is.

Take a person who is used to making $5,000 per month and then loses her source of income. When a new source of income shows up, it doesn't take long before she is back to $5,000 per month. Her money blueprint is set at $5,000 per month.

Those who have challenges with money usually don't know anything about having a money blueprint. That doesn't mean they don't have one. Their preconditioned beliefs and their exposure to people around them sets their money blueprint. You have heard it said that people's net worth is on par with those they live around and hang out with. Their money blueprints are being set by their surroundings.

Taking control of your money blueprint is the key to making more money. There are three simple steps to quickly taking control of your money blueprint:

• Know you have one and determine where it is set
• Reset it in believable steps
• When you reset it, write it down as an "I am" statement

Here's an example: Ask yourself how much money you are used to making in a month. Chances are, that is where your blueprint is currently set. Reset that monthly amount at a higher, but believable amount and write it down.

If you are used to making $5,000 per month and you reset your money blueprint at $1,000,000 per month, chances are your conscious mind will not allow that message to penetrate the subconscious. It is simply too unbelievable. You may say, "I am making $1,000,000 per month," but your conscious thinking takes over with too much negativity on that statement. Remember, your subconscious does not know the difference between what is real and imagined, but in this example, the subconscious may never receive the $1,000,000 message. The conscious goes into overload with doubt and disbelief on that message.

No need to worry; you simply set it too high. If you are used to making $5,000 per month and you reset your money blueprint at $20,000 per month, chances are your conscious thinking will not rebel on you. It may not totally believe it, and it may not know how you are going to get there, but it won't rebel. Your subconscious will receive the message and begin the manifestation process.

After doing this myself and working with thousands of people in training events and personal coaching, I have found you can usually reset your money blueprint at three to four times what you are currently making and your subconscious will get the message. In my own life I have reset my monthly income blueprint four times, and I currently make ten times what I did when I started. It works. Always have a monthly-income amount written as one of your "I am" statements along with other financial goals of your choosing.

LESSON #5: YOU CANNOT THINK YOUR WAY TO ABUNDANCE. YOU MUST FEEL YOUR WAY TO ABUNDANCE.

You do not have to *have* an abundance to attract abundance, but you do have to feel abundant. Any feeling of *lack* of abundance causes a *feeling* that does not allow abundance. If you *feel* abundance, you will send out to *yourself* and to *others* to *give*. If you feel a *lack of abundance*, you will send out to yourself and to others to *get*.

How do I feel financial abundance?

This is a great question, especially when you have an empty bank account and bills are stacking up. It's never about how much money you have; it's about how much money you believe, expect, and feel you can have or obtain. Just ask Donald Trump, who had billions, lost it all through bad real estate ventures, but gained back billions in a few short years. Why? Trump feels, believes, and expects billions, whether it's there or not. That is his financial blueprint. Billions. Law of Attraction kicks in and vibrationally pulls the billions to him. Ask 90 percent of lottery winners who won millions only to lose it and go back to their old lifestyles in a few short years. Why? Because they did not feel, believe, or expect to be worth the millions they gained. Again, Law of Attraction kicks in, and they vibrationally pull their financial blueprint to them, which in this case is a lack of money.

So how do you shift from a poverty blueprint to an abundance blueprint? Simple. Your subconscious mind needs to feel abundance—any abundance. It does not even have to be money. It just needs to feel abundance. Here are some ideas for feeling abundance:

- Focus on the blessings you enjoy in your life. Good health, great relationships, fond memories, anything.
- What you send out you get back, so send out your time, money, or talents simply to reach out. This tells your subconscious mind that you have plenty to give.
- Get yourself a checkbook and start writing out large checks for things you desire as if you really have the money in your account. If you want a $25,000 Harley-Davidson, visit the dealer, write out the check, and act as if it is real. Put it in your journal or a safe place. Remember, your subconscious mind does not know the difference between what is real and imagined, so imagine away.
- Walk outside and look at the abundance of leaves on the trees, the stars in the sky, or blades of grass in your lawn. Bask in

the abundance you see. Again, your mind simply needs to feel abundance.

- Write down and read your "I am" statements. Have statements such as "I am attracting wealth in abundance," "Everything I touch turns to gold," "I am financially independent and free." This is throwing the right tennis balls to yourself over and over again.

- Expose yourself to the lifestyle you desire. Visit the dealerships where your dream car, bike, or boat is.

- Hang out with wealthy people. Go to workshops and seminars where you can be around those who have acquired wealth. I guarantee you will find them at personal-development events.

- Drive through affluent neighborhoods. Admire the beautiful homes you see. Imagine yourself living in one of those homes if that is what you desire.

I recall driving through an affluent neighborhood about ten years ago and past a beautiful home where I saw, through the front window, a guy working at his desk in a beautiful den. I decided right then and there that someday, I would be working in the den of my dream home and someone would drive by, look in, and see me. Just a few weeks before this writing, I was in the den of our new dream home. I was actually working on this book on my new MacBook Pro computer. It was dark outside. My lights were on, and the shutters on my windows were wide open. As I was typing I looked up and saw a car driving slowly in front of our home. They stopped directly in front of my window and looked in at me. I instantly thought of that moment ten years earlier.

The stories in your mind do become the stories of your life, and it's a whole lot of fun when you create the stories you desire.

Note to the Naysayers

You can laugh about this if you want. You can joke and make fun of it if you want. You can also stay where you are in your life—if you want. I put this note in here because I cannot tell you how many people have, literally, laughed at me when I told them that creating financial abundance is really this simple. Laughed at me.

Here is what I do know: I know I have done everything suggested so far in this chapter. I know it created amazing results in record time in my life. I have family members that come over to my home and ask me how I did it. How is it that I can afford all the toys, the travel, the vehicles, the home? They always mention those things they can see. I tell them it is simple: If you feel abundance, you manifest abundance. It is that simple.

How do I create financial abundance?

Simply feel abundance, allow abundance to flow, reset your money blueprint, and have a vehicle and a daily process of action. Remember, balance between affirmation and action is the key to your success. I am fortunate to be in a business where I have a vehicle for creating wealth. I have the opportunity to share that vehicle along with a daily action plan to hundreds of thousands of people. That vehicle is in alignment with who I am as a person, which allows me to create wealth in abundance at a record pace. I encourage you to find your vehicle and make sure it is in alignment with who you are. Once you have that, get to work and have fun along the way.

LESSON #6: ADJUST YOUR LANGUAGE SO ABUNDANCE CAN FLOW

I need money to pay the bills *replaced with* The bills are being paid.

How will I pay the mortgage *replaced with* I sure enjoy my new home.

How can I make more money *replaced with* I'm helping people and adding value.

We need more funds *replaced with* The funds are flowing in.

How do I get out of debt *replaced with* My debts are being paid off.

We sure need a new car *replaced with* I love the smell of my new leather seats.

I was not meant for wealth *replaced with* I enjoy what my wealth allows me to do.

I will never afford that *replaced with* It's nice having the things I want.

I have to make sacrifices *replaced with* I have the opportunity.

I would suggest you never say the words "I can't afford it." Wipe that sentence out of your vocabulary. Replace that with "I choose not to spend my money on that at this time." This is a huge difference, especially to your subconscious where all things are manifested.

(Note: This is now the third time I have mentioned this line in this book. Editors would call that being redundant and act like that's a bad thing. I would also say it is redundant, but I think that is a good thing. Why? Because you, the reader, need to remember it. This simple adjustment of language has made it so I can afford what I want.)

I would also suggest you never use the word "sacrifice." Sacrifice means I have to do things so I can get things. With this mindset you are sending out to get. Opportunity means I get to do things, so I can have things happen for myself and others. With this mindset you are sending out to give.

LESSON #7: NOBODY OWES YOU ANYTHING

The universe and the people in it owe you nothing. You owe it to yourself to give the universe, and the people in it, everything. Remember, you are sending out to give, which means you act as if you already have. Find out who you are and then give yourself away.

LESSON #8: LEARN FROM THE BILLIONAIRES

When you look at the lives of people like Jon Huntsman, O.C. Tanner, Donald Trump, Dale Carnegie, George Bush, Ronald Reagan, and many others, you find a common thread tying them together: They consistently send personal cards and letters to people. In fact, George Bush Sr. attributes the sending of thank-you cards as the single biggest reason he was elected President of the United States.

There is tremendous power in sending written messages to the people in our lives. Not only does it strengthen our network and give us the support we need for success, but it also generates the positive energy needed to attract extraordinary results in our life. You deserve exactly what you send out. Those who send positive messages and written notes of appreciation will receive those things back tenfold.

In addition to sending written messages, billionaires and successful people have learned that wealth is available in abundance. They all have a sense of wealth consciousness that generates wealth in their lives. For you and me to attract wealth we need to accept that there is an abundant supply. There is no need to hoard or protect what we think is our share of the take. This attitude only attracts the scarcity of income and opportunity. Wealthy people have learned they can get anything they want in life if they help enough other people get what they want.

Wealth is, indeed, in abundant supply. When we add value to the marketplace, we tap into this abundant supply. When we carry with us an attitude of abundant thinking, that supply begins to flow to us at a rapid and exciting pace. We become wealth conscious, and we attract people into our lives that are wealth conscious. It is important that we align ourselves with people who attract and generate success and who think in terms of abundance.

THE MOST IMPORTANT LESSON OF ALL

Be you!

Act on that inner prompting that tells you who you are. I am a writer, a speaker, an entertainer, and a CEO. I have found I make the most money when I am writing, speaking, entertaining, and running my business ventures. If I ever feel like my wealth momentum is slowing down, I sit down and write. I plan for the next event. I do who I am. This always brings the wealth momentum back where it needs to be.

Be you!

Do who you are. Always be moving upward and onward with new possibilities.

I like how Abraham Maslow says it: "A musician must make music, an artist must paint, a poet must write, if he is to be ultimately at peace with himself."

Reading through my journal the other day, I came upon this passage:

> "I choose to celebrate every day by exploring new
> possibilities. I will not tear down; I will build up. I
> will not be critical; I will be productive. I will not
> be a pro at what is wrong; I will be a pro at what is
> right. I choose to stay in a creative mindset, always
> brainstorming, always exploring new opportunities,
> and always building. I will spend my time with those

*who do the same thing. **"Upward and onward"** is the motto I choose to live by every day. I choose to live in abundance. I notice the beautiful blue sky, the abundance of leaves on the trees, the abundance of goodness in the world, the smiles instead of the frowns, the laughter and the feel-good emotions that are everywhere. I am a money magnet. I attract wealth in abundance because there is an abundant supply. I continually add value to the market place with who I am. I gladly share my wealth of knowledge, time, talent, and money with those who are in need. I had a starting point, and I was mentored along the way. I recognize everyone has a starting point, and I am there to give back that which was given to me. I celebrate the genius within everyone I meet. Talents, gifts, and abilities are flowing from the hearts and minds of everyone around me."*

These are the thoughts that go through the mind of a wealth-conscious person. Everyone has the ability to think like this. When these thoughts come to you, write them down. You will cherish them forever.

One of my biggest heroes is Norman Vincent Peale. He said it like this:

> *"We are here to be excited from youth to old age, to have an insatiable curiosity about the world. We are also here to help others by practicing a friendly attitude, and every person is born for a purpose. Everyone has a God-given potential, in essence, built into them, and if we are to live life to its fullest, we must realize that potential."*

"Love leaves a legacy. How you treat other people is the most enduring impact you can leave on earth."

RICK WARREN

"I will greet this day with love in my heart. I will love the sun for it warms my bones; yet I will love the rain for it cleanses my spirit. I will love the light for it shows me the way; yet I will love the darkness for it shows me the stars. I will welcome happiness for it enlarges my heart; yet I will endure sadness for it opens my soul."

OG MANDINO

CHAPTER 14

Love in Abundance

I wrote the following passage in my journal early one morning:

> *"Love is the highest form of energy in the universe. Through love of ourselves, love for others, love for our surroundings, love for our opportunities, love for all possibilities, and, yes, even love for our challenges, we can stay in the vibrational energy of creation. It is through creation that abundance flows. It is through love that creation is possible."*

Now, think about the infinite flow of energy:

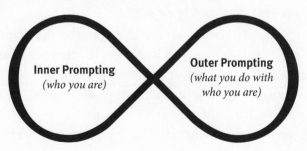

Inner Prompting
(who you are)

Outer Prompting
(what you do with who you are)

It teaches us that by acting on our inner promptings (who we are) and our outer promptings (what we do with who we are), we create this flow of positive energy.

By understanding our uniqueness, our purpose, and our possibilities (who we are), we activate our inner guide and take control of our destiny.

By reaching out to others with love, compassion, respect, and understanding (what we do with who we are), we make the difference in the world that only we can make.

LOVE IS THE KEY

Love is the key to making this work. Love for self and others generates love for surroundings and opportunities. Love for self and others generates love for possibilities and challenges. Love is the driving energy behind every positive creation in the universe. Love is what makes the infinite flow of energy work. Love is what makes everything positive work.

You cannot be in a negative mindset and maintain a feeling of love at the same time. Anything that takes you away from the feeling of love should be avoided. Anything that draws you to the feeling of love should be pursued.

FIND WHAT YOU LOVE AND STICK WITH IT

I love to read, I love to write, I love to teach, I love music, and I love people. Whenever my focus is on those five things, I prosper in all areas of my life. Find what you love and stick with it. When you walk into our home, the left side of the entryway is our library full of books we have accumulated over the past thirty years. On the right side of the entry is the den where I use my desk, computer, and files for writing and reflecting. I love this entryway because it is a visual of the things I love and have stuck with over the years.

On our walls throughout the home, we have pictures of people and events. I love the people in these pictures. They inspire me.

In our library I have journals full of stories about people I have met and who have become lifelong friends. As I read these journal entries I am filled with joy because those stories represent something that I love: people. I have considered it a great blessing in my life to have a love for people. I have created memories with people who have shaped who I am as a person today.

When I focus on my love for people, my inner and outer promptings flow like a running faucet. The infinite flow of energy is running in high gear, and I am reaping the benefits of prosperous living as a result. Love for others is the most powerful source for keeping yourself in the flow of your promptings.

If you don't love people, *start*! Change your "I am" statements to reflect a love for self and others and watch what happens. If you do love people, then *love them more*! Create "I am" statements that expand your network of friends and associates. Celebrate the people you meet with pictures, gifts, and the written word. Send them birthday cards because they deserve to be celebrated. Capture moments in their lives with pictures and share those pictures with them. Celebrate the diversity existing in the world today. Realize people are different for a reason. Our differences make things exciting. Learn to accept people for who they are, love them for who they are, and celebrate them for being them.

THE BROTHER WITHIN

I have a dear friend named Linda Clemons. She is a vibrant and beautiful African-American woman from Indiana. Linda was attending one of our events with her friend Melinda. I was on stage dancing and singing rap music and sharing words of inspiration with all the passion I had. Melinda leaned over and whispered in Linda's ear, "There's a little black man just waiting to jump out of Kody." They both laughed and shared that story with me later. While sharing that story, Linda said she had a new nickname for me. She called me "the brother within."

Now, I have lots of titles and names I go by in life, but I can think of none that makes me feel better than that one. It does represent who I am: a simple white boy who cares about and loves people regardless of race, color, or ethnicity. In fact, when I am with my friends who appear to be different than me, I genuinely want to be accepted by them. They have personality traits and experiences I would like to acquire. I love the passion, creativity, and rhythm that comes from my black friends. I love the sensitivity and graciousness that comes from my Asian friends. I love the sense of family and brotherhood that comes from my Hispanic and Latino friends. I love the conviction and commitment that comes from my Jewish friends. I love the jovial and kickback nature that comes from my friends "down under." I love the courage and the emotion that comes from my friends who have chosen lifestyles different than my own. I accept them all for who they are and, because of that, I know they accept me too.

This is energy, folks. This is the stuff that makes the world go around. Love for self and others is the true test we have to pass as human beings, and it is the greatest source of energy in the universe. There are many more groups of people I have not had the opportunity to meet and add as part of my history. I look forward to meeting and being friends with all types of people from every walk of life.

WHERE THE "BROTHER WITHIN" CAME FROM

Twenty-five years ago I was serving as a Christian missionary in Washington, D.C., and Baltimore, Maryland. This was the perfect place for me to serve because people from everywhere in the world lived there. I was introduced to the diversity of culture and tradition the people of this world offer, and I loved the experience.

During this time of service I was asked to move from Springfield, Virginia, to Baltimore, Maryland. In Virginia I was working with people from America, Cambodia, Laos, and Thailand. In Baltimore I would be working primarily with African Americans from the inner city. Though I was sad to leave my new friends in Virginia, I was excited to meet new ones in Baltimore. My church leader gave me keys to a car, introduced me to a new missionary I would be training, gave me a map and an address for our apartment, and waved goodbye. I had never been to Baltimore in my life. I knew nothing about it. We drove thirty miles due north from the Virginia side of the Potomac River to our new home in Baltimore.

When we arrived, we threw our suitcases in our apartment and immediately went out to walk the neighborhoods. The first street we visited was McCabe Avenue, right in the heart of inner-city Baltimore. It quickly became obvious that white people were not seen much there. The first question we were asked was if we were lost or had taken a wrong turn somewhere. When we answered no, the initial reaction was not the most friendly. For the first time in my life I discovered what it felt like to be the minority, and it didn't feel that great. I was determined to become part of this neighborhood regardless of the color of my skin.

Within the first several days we met a seventeen-year-old black kid named Tony Watson. Tony and I became instant friends. Fortunately for us, Tony was like a ringleader on the streets. Everyone liked Tony, and if we were with him, we were OK. This was in 1984. This is when rap music was beginning to make a name for itself, and many of the kids on the street were bustin' out the rhymes. In fact, back then they had the turntables on their porches, and they would mix their music and rap on the street corners. I thought this was one of the coolest things I had ever seen. I told Tony I wanted him to teach me how to rap. He and his buddies would joke about the white boy rapping, but they did teach me, and we rapped on the street corners together.

To this day I have carried with me a love for rap music. It reminds me of a seventeen-year-old black boy accepting a twenty-year-old white boy for who I was. To honor Tony, I sing rap music at most seminars and events I conduct. We have lots of fun with this. In fact, I have an exercise where I get the whole audience involved singing part of a rap song with me. Energy is always high, and we have a great time with it.

The following is a rap song we do at our Treat'em Right seminars for SendOutCards, highlighting many of the benefits and features the program provides.

> We're still sending out cards, because we know who we
> are, rockin' to the beat of Kody B.
> Watch out, stand back, eagle take flight, let me take you
> on a tour of the website.
> Gift account, gift give 'em away, an unexpected card,
> send it out every day.
> I said sending out a message, telling how you feel, just
> push the send button, it ain't no big deal.
> Add a picture, celebrate life, reaching on out from a
> husband to his wife.
> Little kids love to get a card, get it done, boy, it just ain't
> that hard.
> Thoughts, feelings, actions and deeds, takin' on care of all
> of your people's needs.

*Everybody sing "S" because we're on the beat now, "O,"
got to give a gift a week now, "C," people get you on
your feet now, "SOC"*

*Everybody sing "S" because we're on the beat now, "O,"
got to give a gift a week now, "C," people get you on
your feet now, "SOC"*

*A card a day, now a gift a week, staying on your game
while you turn the other cheek.*

*Send to get, no, send to give, do it every day and you will
start to live.*

*I said celebrate life and celebrate it now, givin' 'em a gift
account until they say wow wow, PicturePlus, it is the
bomb, photo on the front and send it to your mom.*

*Add a caption, a word bubble too, finish with a border
and they will say woo-woo.*

*Self-promotion, it's for the birds, I said appreciation wins
with a card and simple words.*

*Everybody sing "S" because we're on the beat now, "O,"
got to give a gift a week now, "C," people get you on
your feet now, "SOC"*

*Everybody sing "S" because we're on the beat now, "O,"
got to give a gift a week now, "C," people get you on
your feet now, "SOC"*

*Have a prompting, time to act, do it every day and you
will be jacked.*

Stand tall, send out, be cool.

Getting in the flow with your card-sending tool.

Changing lives one card at a time, I said keep it on going
because you're doing just fine.
Collect a story, make it two or three, dreams coming
true, be the best you can be.
I said "I am" statements, they make you click, you are a
cool guy and you're a hot chick.
Be an eagle, soar high in the blue.
Know your big picture and it will come true.

Everybody sing "S" because we're on the beat now, "O,"
got to give a gift a week now, "C," people get you on
your feet now, "SOC"
Everybody sing "S" because we're on the beat now, "O,"
got to give a gift a week now, "C," people get you on
your feet now, "SOC"
Everybody say "S"............... "O".................. "C"
"SOC" yeah!

I guess now you can appreciate why Linda Clemons calls me the "brother within."

ONE OF MY MOST CHERISHED POSSESSIONS

Lots has happened since the days on the streets of Baltimore. However, as you can see, I have stuck with what I love. When I rap, I am using my love of music and cherishing memories of people I love from the streets of Baltimore. Having fun with this rap music is a way for me to trigger the positive energy I had with those people, and it makes me feel good. It also celebrates the love of self and others.

If you remember, when we first walked down McCabe Avenue, we were not well accepted. When I left those streets, I left the presence of some of the greatest friends I will ever have. One of those friends was Sharon Harding. She was an adorable African-American lady who lived with her mother Elsie. Sharon and Elsie were great examples to me. They were like my moms away from home. They always made me feel good.

When I left Baltimore, Sharon gave me a gift to remember her by. It was one of her most prized possessions, and she wanted me to have it. It was a little black Cabbage Patch doll named Gus. When she gave this to me, she said, "I want you to have this because if I would have ever had my own son, I would have wanted him to be like you." Those words meant the world to me. I guess I really am the "brother within."

McCABE AVENUE 25 YEARS LATER

Twenty-five years later—ironically, on Martin Luther King Jr. Day and on the eve of the inauguration of our first black president in America—I drove down to McCabe Avenue. I parked the rental car on the same street corner where Tony and I sang those rap songs so many years ago. Everything was exactly the same. It was as if time had stood still. This was a magical moment for me. The memories, along with all their emotions, flooded back to me. It was snowing, and young black children were playing in the streets just like I remembered so long ago. The homes looked exactly the same. It was at this moment that I realized how much McCabe Avenue and its surrounding neighborhoods defined who I am today as a person.

I truly love the people I served in Baltimore. I love their fun nature, their ability to be creative and happy in adverse living conditions, their amazing faith, and their love for life. I had the priceless opportunity to become friends with African Americans, Nigerians, Haitians, Cambodians, Vietnamese, Laotions, and people from every part of the world.

I loved them all. I wanted to be like them, become a part of their world. I wanted to be accepted as one of them and, in most cases, I was.

My friends from Cambodia call me *Dadavood*. It means *always happy*.

My friends from Laos call me *Sooksun*. It means *happy eyes*.

My African American friends call me "the brother within." They say there is a little black boy just wanting to jump out of me.

Those are three of the most cherished compliments I have ever been given.

My missionary experience taught me we are blessed with numerous ethnic groups, but there is only one race. It's called the "human race." We are all brothers and sisters in this game called Life, and we can learn so much from each other. I believe that becoming united as people is the true test we need to pass as human beings. If we figure out how to do that, we enhance our life experience more than you can imagine.

So here I am in my life journey. It has been twenty-five years since the amazing days of rapping on the streets of Baltimore with my friend Tony Watson. I am now a CEO of a fast-growing company and a motivational speaker. When I take to the stage, I am known to throw the bling on and bust out some rhymes. I am Kody B, the master MC. I don't do this because I think I'm cool (even though I am). I do this to pay tribute to my friend Tony. I do this because it celebrates ethnic diversity; it represents the story of a seventeen-year-old black kid who accepted a twenty-year-old white kid for who he was.

We are fortunate to be living at a higher spiritual level today than we were twenty-five years ago. The self-help section of the bookstore is larger than ever, and seminars and lectures are widespread on positive affirmation and Law of Attraction principles. We are seeing more and more non-denominational movements where the barriers of religion are coming down, and people are accepting love, relationship, and spirituality at record levels. We are a kinder, gentler people, and we are awakening to new possibility. Our world is becoming smaller, and our social networks are becoming larger.

We are rich in ethnic diversity and strong in our resolve to be as one group, one family, and one race. Together we are becoming better people, and united, we are sending out that goodness to the world.

Many have paved the way before us, many who committed their lives to the cause of freedom and equality. I am fascinated by the life of the late Dr. Martin Luther King, Jr. Following the example of Mahatma Gandhi, Dr. King led a crusade of non-violent protest against the evils of segregation and inequality for people of color. I have had the chance to read his articles and speeches. It is there that you learn the power and passion of this man. You also learn the significance of his philosophy and leadership and the dramatic impact it had on the history of the world.

In his speeches Dr. King continually taught the non-violent philosophy by explaining three types of love. The first is *eros*, the romantic type of love between two people. The second is *theos*, the friendship or commonality connection between people. The third type was the central theme of his non-violent philosophy. It is *agape*, the love for the sake of loving—the unconditional aspect of loving the person and disliking bad or unkind behavior.

This is the kind of love that will accelerate your infinite flow of energy. This is the kind of love that nourishes the inner and outer promptings of your life and guides you to your genius within.

UNITED WE SEND

All these stories represent my experience with people I have met and loved throughout my life. Fortunately for me, my group of friends are rich in ethnic diversity. I have learned so much from all of them. To pay tribute to those friendships and memories, I produced a song titled "United We Send." I have included the words below. The song itself is a ballad and rap mix telling the story of my experiences on McCabe Avenue.

"United We Send" (ballad)

*Our world is blessed with numerous ethnic groups of
  people
But there is only one race, and it's called the human race
We are all brothers and sisters in this game called life
And we can learn so much from each other*

*I believe that becoming united as a people is the true test
  we need to pass as human beings
To do this we must believe in a world that is rich in
  ethnic diversity and united in our resolve to be one
  group, one family, and one race
We are united as a people, and united we send out who
  we are to the world
United we send, together we are, it's not what you do,
  it's what you do with who you are.
United we send, together we'll be, I'll learn from you
  and you will learn from me*

*Here is a story of a boy in the 'hood
On the corner of McCabe is where he stood*

Brothers and sisters all around
And looking different is what he found

But looks didn't matter, his inner voice said
Titles and labels, nothing one can't shed
Standing tall it was time to win
A white boy, yes, but a brother within

United we send, together we are, it's not what you do,
  it's what you do with who you are.
United we send, together we'll be, I'll learn from you
  and you will learn from me

(rap mix)

Learning from me, you know I'm chillin' in the hood
My friends from Cambodia, they call me dadavood
It means I'm happy, I'm living life for what it can be
Celebrating differences of you and me

Can't you see McCabe Avenue the place is where I
  belong?
Lovin' and be lovin' is the way we get along
It's how we knowin' right from wrong
So listen to the song
It's who you are that makes you strong
It is the song of togetherness

We are as one
My people from Laos, yes, they call me sooksun

It's happy eyes for everyone
Latinos, Hispanics, Asians, Indians
We all come together and we all live as one

(ballad)

One more time, new destination
Celebrate colors, a joyous occasion
Song and dance, rhythm and sound
Rich in diversity is what he found

Loving people for who they are
Everyone wishes upon a star
United we send, together we'll be
I will learn from you and you will learn from me
Sending out love, sending hope and devotion
Brothers and sisters, united in motion
United we are as boys and girls
United we send out who we are to the world

United we send, together we are, it's not what you do, it's
*   what you do with who you are.*
United we send, together we'll be, I'll learn from you
*   and you will learn from me*

LOVE IN ABUNDANCE

Love is in abundant supply. In fact, love is what creates abundance. Love is the fuel that drives your infinite flow of energy. I encourage you to find what you love and stick with it. Make sure other people are on that list. As you celebrate your own life and the lives of others, your love will grow, and your promptings will flow.

"There is only one success—to be able to spend your life in your own way."

CHRISTOPHER MORLEY

"There is one thing that an eagle instinctively knows; it flies or it dies."

KODY BATEMAN

"With every pursuit for excellence in life, remember, Always an Eagle."

KRISTOPHER A. BATEMAN

CHAPTER 15

Always an Eagle

I started this book by telling the story about my brother who was killed when he was twenty-nine years old. We talked about his greatness as a brother, a son, a husband, and a father. In his short twenty-nine years on this earth Kris made a significant impact in the lives of many people. You could say he left a legacy for many of us to follow.

Following the example of our father, Kris decided he wanted to become an Eagle Scout. Once Kris decided anything, you could consider it done because that was the way he was. He achieved the rank of Eagle at the age of thirteen. This is the youngest possible age to achieve the highest rank in Boy Scouts. Following his example, my older brother Kelly decided he would also become an Eagle Scout. With the help of Kris and many others Kelly also achieved this rank at a young age.

Along comes me. My goodness, I didn't really like scouting that much, but it became very clear that Bateman boys were Eagles. Following the example of my father and my brothers, I too became an Eagle Scout.

To become an Eagle, you are required to do an Eagle Scout project that benefits the community and its residents. Kris, Kelly, and I all conducted the same project at different times. We had a swimming pool at our home, and each of us taught swimming lessons to young children in the neighborhood. This was my first experience at teaching a skill to others, and I really enjoyed it. To this day I choose swimming as my primary form of exercise because it reminds me of what I shared in common with my Eagle brothers.

When you receive your Eagle badge, the scout leaders pin an Eagle badge on the scout and an Eagle pin on the mother of the scout. My dad says they do that because the mother does most of the work anyway. When the scout receives this honor, he is invited to join what they call an Eagle's Nest. Anyone in attendance at an Eagle Scout court of honor who has ever earned the rank of Eagle is invited to sit in that "nest." Their job is to represent all Eagles and welcome the new Eagle to the nest after he has been pinned with the badge. I was welcomed into the Eagle's Nest by my father, my brother Kris, and my brother Kelly. I will always remember that moment.

Kris is the brother who set the example. He believed that becoming an Eagle was a challenging milestone that turned boys into men. He also believed Eagles would always be Eagles, meaning they would go on to accomplish whatever they set their mind to.

At the age of twenty Kris became what they call a scoutmaster. He was a leader of a troop of scouts, and his job was to help them through the ranks until they achieved the highest honor of Eagle. To this day I hear stories from many of Kris's scouts about how he changed their lives, gave them hope, and helped them believe in themselves. All those scouts are now grown men with families and legacies of their own.

Kris used to always say, "Once an Eagle, always an Eagle." When a new scout started in Kris's program, he would present the boy with a certificate including the new scout's name and the words, "Always an Eagle." He was treating that new scout as if he had already obtained the highest rank in the scouting program. I mentioned earlier in this book the power of the "I am" statement is that you already are those things you write down. Those boys were Eagles from Day One. Is it any wonder the majority of the boys in Kris's program became Eagle Scouts?

Becoming an Eagle does not just apply to a young man in the scouting program. Anyone can become an Eagle. The Eagle represents greatness. Every human being has greatness in them.

WHAT IT MEANS TO BE AN EAGLE!

Eagles soar higher than the rest of the world. Eagles are majestic; they provide beauty and direction for all of us to follow. *Eagles get what they want from life,* and they are an inspiration.

We all have the opportunity to become as eagles. This means we too can provide beauty and direction for others to follow. *This means we too will get what we want from life* and, as a result, be an inspiration to many.

Eagles have a different view on the world than others. Eagles fly high above where they view the big picture of life and see all the beauties of the world. Eagles have incredible vision. They can spot a fish under water from a thousand feet in the air. They tune in on that fish and make it their goal. With their eyes firmly focused they soar down from the skies and grab their fish from the water. This is one of the most beautiful things to witness in nature.

I recently attended an Eagle Scout court of honor where a live bald eagle was brought into the room. This was a beautiful creature. She was perched on the forearm of her trainer. When they took the blinders from her eyes, she looked around the room as if she was scoping out her new territory. This eagle would make piercing eye contact with people in the room. It was amazing. I was sitting about thirty feet away, and this eagle made eye contact with me. She kept her eyes focused on my eyes for several seconds. I was spellbound.

That eagle taught me a valuable lesson that night. She taught me the importance of eye contact. We need to look people in the eye and express a caring feeling in our gaze.

EAGLE OBSERVATIONS

The trainer shared some interesting information about eagles. They are loyal to one partner throughout their lives. They migrate thousands of miles every fall and return to the exact same location every year; often they find the exact same tree. This takes incredible focus.

Eagles soar higher by spreading their wings and allowing the winds to push them upward. An enemy to the eagle is a crow. A crow will fly around an eagle and bother it with obnoxious noises. The eagle will spread its wings, find an updraft in the wind, and soar in a circular motion higher and higher until the crow can no longer follow it. Eagles have been seen as high as 20,000 feet in the air. Eagles soar higher than any other bird by allowing nature to lift them upward. Other birds will flap their wings wildly in order to take flight. The interesting thing is that the harder they flap, the lower they fly. As an example, a chicken flaps its wings the hardest and flies the lowest. An eagle flaps its wings with effortless grace and ease and flies the highest.

Another interesting thing about eagles is how they train their young. When the eaglet is still at a very young age—about three months old—the mother will begin to prepare it for its first flight. She will train the young eaglet to flap its wings in the nest, and she will begin to withhold food and make the nest more uncomfortable.

Most of the time the eagle's nest is high above the ground in the top of a tree or along a cliff's edge. Before the young eagle has ever taken flight, the mother will persuade or even push her young eaglet off the edge of the nest. The young eaglet will drop rapidly towards the ground while flapping his wings wildly. If the eaglets do not take flight, their mothers or fathers will fly down and scoop them up just before they hit the ground.

They have been known to do this several times before the eaglet flies solo. Ironically it is when the young eaglet learns to spread its wings and soar that he safely takes flight on his own. With the speed of the fall and the force of the wind beneath the newly stretched wings, the young eagle naturally is lifted upward to its first flight.

That may seem like a harsh way to train your young. After all, they have been comfortable in their nest, dependent on their mother to nurture, feed, and protect them. All of a sudden the mother pushes that cute little eaglet off the edge and allows it to drop to what could be an apparent sudden death. But the eagle knows what an eaglet is capable of. The eagle also knows that an eaglet must fly on its own to survive. An eaglet must claim its natural grace and independence or it will die. Better to take a chance by pushing their young than to coddle them into a life of dependence and failure. An eaglet is not an eagle unless it flies.

SO WHAT DOES IT MEAN TO BE AN EAGLE?

It means we view the world differently than others. It means we strive to find the big picture and reap the benefits of that view. It means we are focused on the things we want in life, and we pursue them with tenacity. It means we make eye contact with others because we care about them, we are intrigued by them, and we are interested in them. It means we allow success to flow, and we do not stick around to listen to the obnoxious noises of negativity; rather than fight it, we simply soar higher. An eagle always rises above the trials and challenges of life. It does not stick around to bicker, wonder, worry, or force its way to anything. An eagle simply spreads its wings and flies higher.

Many believe eagles sense a storm before it arrives. They will find a place high above the ground to perch themselves as they wait for the storm to arrive. When the winds of the storm appear, the eagle will take flight, spread its wings, and allow the fiery winds to push it upward. As other birds and animals hide from the storm, the eagle sails above it.

WATCH OUT, STAND BACK, EAGLE TAKE FLIGHT

Like an eagle, we can make a decision to take flight with our lives. When that decision is made, those around do need to stand back and watch because it is a miraculous sight. To take flight, there comes a time when you must jump from the nest. If you are lucky, there might be someone who loves you enough to push you out. Remember, if you stay in the nest you die. If you jump from the nest, you fly. It's that simple.

DEFINE YOUR NEST

What is the nest or security blanket you think is protecting you? Is it a job, a relationship, a bad habit, drama, gossip, excuses, blame, complaining, or victimization? You might ask how any of those things could be considered your nest. Think about it. If any of those things are holding you back, that is exactly what you have made them; your little nest you are hoping will protect you. You have made those things the very place you are scared to death to jump from. They become your excuse. You are like the little eaglet shaking, shivering, and scared. If loved ones are pushing you to the edge, you might wonder why they are being so mean to you. It is estimated that as many as 40 percent of young eaglets never take flight. Why? Because they are too scared. What happens to them? They die. They die from the fall of an attempted flight or from predators snatching them up from the ground. Observers believe a determining factor between young eaglets who survive or die is their level of confidence. Some eaglets appear to be more aggressive and willing to venture out of the nest. Others want Mama to keep feeding them.

ARE YOU GOING TO BE AN EAGLET THAT DIES OR AN EAGLE THAT FLIES?

If you want to be an eagle that flies, then it is time to wake up and realize it is up to you. You cannot keep riding on the wings of whatever security blanket you have created for yourself. It's time for the excuses to stop and the action to start. This process is a journey, and many of us are at different levels of this journey. Some of you reading this may be at the very beginning, full of excuses, blame, and anything else you are clinging to. That is OK as long as you are willing to recognize that and begin moving away from it. Others are further along. Many of you have already made transformations and taken charge of your life. You have gone through the process of shedding the excuses, and you are jumping from the nest and taking flight. I would like to challenge you as well.

I am fortunate to work with thousands of people who are midway on this journey. They are serious about their personal development, and they make a conscious effort to take flight. I have found that this midway point can be a challenging place as well. Many who have taken flight will fall to the temptation of negativity and find their way back to their nest, where they cling to its edges. The scariest part of this is they often don't know they are doing it. After all, they already know how to take charge, they already know how to shed excuses and take flight, they have already jumped from the nest, spread their wings and flown high. How could they possibly be back in their nest clinging to its edges for dear life?

It happens all the time, and I am here to tell you that the simple difference between a crow's flight and an eagle's flight is found right here. A crow can fly. In fact, a crow flies really well. On the other hand, an eagle soars higher. An eagle is majestic and provides beauty and direction for all to follow. A crow is OK; an eagle is magnificent.

The line between OK and magnificent is very thin. Magnificence comes from those who take flight and soar every day, like an eagle. Magnificence comes from those who immediately recognize when they begin to cling to the nest. They shake the temptation and, again, take flight. Magnificence comes from those who are consistent in their determination to be majestic, to soar higher, to be an example, to live life to its fullest potential. This is what eagles do, and this is what you can do.

The single biggest factor between being OK and being magnificent is taking full responsibility for what you are experiencing. I work in a business where people are paid based on the amount of sales volume they and their downline organizations create. I love this business because it pays you exactly what you are worth. If your organization duplicates and produces, you get paid. If it doesn't, you don't. It's that simple.

I can tell the difference between OK and magnificence based on how our representatives answer this question:

My sales volume is up or down because _____?

If their answer points the finger to anything or anyone besides themselves, they are OK. If their answer includes personal responsibility, they are magnificent.

I can tell another difference between OK and magnificence based on whether or not our representatives use the following response:

Yeah, but?

Yeah, but the economy is down.

Yeah, but you don't understand what we are going through.

Yeah, but so-and-so keeps messing up.

Yeah, but they keep making mistakes.

Yeah, but I could do it better.

On and on.

Let me make one thing perfectly clear: There are no "Yeah, buts" with personal responsibility.

If an eagle comes back to its nest without dinner, do you think any "yeah, buts" are going to matter? Can you imagine the eagle saying, "Yeah, but the wind was blowing too hard," or "Yeah, but the rabbit was running too fast," or "Yeah, but the fish was too deep in the water"? Any eagle or eaglet sitting in the nest at that moment could care less about any "yeah, buts" — they don't have dinner.

Excuses and fault-finding have never built or accomplished anything. An eagle does nothing but explore possibilities. An eagle is, by far, the most successful hunter in the wilderness. No other predator even comes close. However, an eagle still only succeeds with a kill 50 percent of the time. That means that one out of every two times it goes on a hunt, the eagle comes back a failure. What does the eagle do? He comes back to his perch and immediately scans his territory for another possibility. Being an eagle means we are always in the mindset of possibility, prepared to take flight without hesitation. An eagle has no time to make excuses or find fault. The eagle is too busy exploring and acting on possibility.

BE AN EAGLE THAT FLIES!

An eagle uses its wings and grace and combines these with the elements of nature to be an eagle. We, as human beings, can use our uniqueness, our gifts, and our abilities along with the elements of nature to be as an eagle.

In this book we have discussed a philosophy that will ensure that we soar as an eagle. The infinite flow of energy around our inner and outer promptings will allow us to experience the grace and elegance of the eagle. By acting on our inner and outer promptings we spread our wings in an effortless flow to soar higher than we ever thought possible.

We become focused on the things we want in life. We learn how to get in the "feel good" of those wants by acting on our promptings and staying in a positive mindset. This helps us to be like eagles. It gives us the focus we need to accomplish our goals and stake claim on the lives we deserve.

By acting on our promptings we stay in the mindset of possibility. As an example, if you have a prompting to say thank you to someone and you act by sending that person a greeting card with a small gift, you are giving who you are to someone who deserves celebration. In that process there is nothing negative, no fault-finding, no excuses, and no complaints. There is nothing but positive, feel-good activity. This is where the mindset of possibility flourishes.

The more you act on your promptings, the more you stay in this infinite flow of energy where your wings are spread and the elements of nature allow you to soar effortlessly upward and onward to new possibility.

It is time for all of us to soar like eagles. "Once an Eagle, always an Eagle." We all have that incredible opportunity to become eagles.

ALWAYS AN EAGLE

In memory of my brother Kris, SendOutCards has a recognition program where its highest rank is eagle. Those who obtain that rank are permanent members of an Eagle's Nest. The Eagle's Nest serves as an advisory board and assists with the strategic direction of our company. Top-performing representatives may also serve as temporary members in the Eagle's Nest prior to them achieving the highest rank of eagle.

I am honored to serve with this nest of eagles. Whether they have yet earned the rank or not, they are serving, acting, and flying as eagles. You have heard it said, "If you want to soar with the eagles, you need to be around them." I am blessed because I am around eagles.

When my brother died, he was wearing a ring with an eagle emblem on it. My father had given Kris that ring; it was a ring Dad made for himself many years before. When his mother died, my dad found his mother's Eagle pin among her belongings. This was the pin she received when my dad received his Eagle Scout award in 1951.

My dad took that pin and had it made into an eagle ring. He did this to remember his mother who had the courage to push him out of the nest and help him become an eagle. My dad wore that ring for many years, right up to the day he presented it to his son Kris.

At the time, Kris was serving as a scoutmaster and was presiding at an Eagle court of honor for one of his scouts. When the court of honor was about to end, my dad had a prompting he needed to give his Eagle ring to my brother Kris. He presented the ring to him, and Kris wore it from that moment until the day he died.

If you remember, Kris was electrocuted on the job. When the electricity went through his body, it left a burn mark on the side of this ring. That ring was preserved and later presented to Kris's oldest son the day he received his Eagle Scout award. Traditions run deep, and you can see our family has created a tradition around the emblem of an eagle. In this chapter you have read what it means to be an eagle. There is so much to be learned by the nature of the eagle. The more we visualize the eagle in our lives, the more we become like them. I guess that is what my dad visualized by the eagle on a ring that he, his son, and his grandson could look down at and see.

To keep that tradition going I was surprised at one of our Send-OutCards national events by having an Eagle ring presented to me by my father; my wife Jodi; my brother Kris's wife Michelle; their three children Kris Jr., Samantha, and Cole; and the SendOutCards reps who were currently serving in the Eagle's Nest. They presented me with an honorary eagle award and gave me an exact replica of the ring my brother was wearing when he died. It even has a marking on the side where the electricity hit and an inscription inside that says, "Always an Eagle."

I was deeply touched and humbled by this honor. I am simply a messenger with a message to act on our promptings and fly like eagles. I am graced with the presence of eagles all around me, people who are great examples to me. When I look down at this ring, I am reminded of all the people in my life that should be honored with this ring. As a result, I am a humble recipient of the eagle ring, and I wear it to represent those around me.

I now wear that ring to visualize the eagle every day of my life. Those who achieve the rank of eagle in SendOutCards also receive a replica of this ring. I encourage everyone to visualize the eagle in your life. By using pictures or jewelry or anything that helps you remember the eagle, you can be in the presence of magnificence.

Everyone is an eagle. We just need to claim it, dare to jump from the nest, and soar as we were meant to soar.

EAGLE ONE HAS LANDED

Prior to receiving this award I wrote an "I am" statement that says, "I am an eagle." I strive to live my life as an eagle, to be a person as described in this chapter. There are days I do really well, and other days I don't. I have strengths and weaknesses as everyone does. I simply strive to be a little better every day. To help me remember that I represent the eagle, I always send a text message to my wife Jodi when I land on the airplanes that fly me around the world. I say, "Eagle One has landed." Jodi always responds with a loving remark that keeps me going in a positive way.

If you are striving to be as an eagle, you already are an eagle. Wear the eagle jewelry, hang the eagle pictures, write the eagle "I am" statements, and send the "Eagle One has landed" text messages to your loved ones because you are an eagle. You will always be an eagle. These simple things will remind you of that every day.

Just before completing the rough draft of this book I had twelve chapters and all the notes for the final three chapters of the book in my laptop computer. Our family took a trip to Lake Powell, and we loaded all our belongings onto our houseboat. We use carts to carry our supplies from the truck across the marina to the slip where the boat sits. In one of those carts we had left my laptop computer.

It was late at night when we discovered the computer was missing. You can imagine the anxiety I felt as years of work was sitting in a lost computer. We searched the marina to no avail. At about midnight I noticed I had a voice mail on my phone from a Colorado phone number. The message was from a lady who had found my computer. I immediately called her, and she told me where her boat was located in the slips. Jodi and I rushed over, and the first thing we noticed was her beautiful forty-two-foot cruiser yacht. You won't believe the name on the back of it—"Eagle One."

When she gave me the computer bag, she said she looked through the bag to find who it might belong to. She noticed I had lots of notes in the bag about being an eagle. She figured whoever owned this computer really needed it because there was something about eagles on it. I vowed at that moment that I would always have something about eagles either written or visualized with me every day of my life. I encourage you to do the same.

"A ship in harbor is safe but that is not

what ships are for."

JOHN A. SHEDD

"Go confidently in the direction of your dreams. Live the life you have imagined."

HENRY DAVID THOREAU

CONCLUSION

A Life Worth Celebrating

My dad often comments that one the greatest fears of parents who lose children is that their son or daughter will be forgotten, that people would soon forget the special person he or she was. He says parents never forget because they adore their children, but what about the rest of the world? Would people remember the amazing person Kris was? Would people follow his example and talk about the legacy he left?

Tearfully my dad says he and my mom will be eternally grateful for the SendOutCards movement for creating this eagle rank and Eagle's Nest in memory of Kristopher Alden Bateman. Dad is deeply grateful for the thousands and soon to be millions of people who honor Kris whereby his legacy will not be forgotten.

I humbly now share with you a final message Kris would be sharing if he were here. This is what he would say:

> *You all have a legacy in you. You all have lives worth celebrating. You all have the opportunity to make a lasting difference in the world. I am honored that many would pay tribute to me as a person who was, and is, an eagle. I am honored that my story*

is told over and over again. I am honored that the words "always an eagle" sit beneath my name. I am grateful for the kindness of so many.

I know that every one of you has the capacity for greatness. I know that every one of you are eagles. There are things in this life only you can do. There are people at certain times in life that only you can touch. You have a life worth celebrating, and I encourage you to celebrate it every day.

I woke up one morning and kissed my wife and three children goodbye before I walked out the door for the last time. I have heard many of you ask if a person knows he is going to die before he does. I can answer that question: I did not know. I did not know that morning would be the last time I would see my family. I went to work; I went to a tennis court to do a job. I spoke to my wife on a two-way radio, and I climbed up on a metal pole. The next thing I knew, I was in a different place. My brother Kody is writing this message for me. You can believe this kind of thing happens or not if you want to, but it is happening right now.

Most of you never knew me, but you pay tribute to me. I encourage you to pay tribute to those you do know—the people you love and share your lives with. Pay tribute to them with your words and your actions. Celebrate yourself for who you are. Celebrate others for who they are. If you do those simple things you will live a life of happiness, and you will be guided to your genius within.

FINAL THOUGHTS

The inner prompting is who you are. The outer prompting is what you do with who you are. These promptings are your guide to making the difference only you can make in the world. Through the passing of my brother Kris, my mother, and others I have been close to, I have learned the amazing value of human life. Through example, my mother taught me to treat all people as if they were my favorite. Through example, Kris taught all of us what it means to be an eagle.

As you close the cover of this book I challenge you to put it somewhere safe on your bookshelf. Walk out your front door and be an eagle. Soar higher than the rest of the world. Be majestic. Provide beauty and direction for all to follow.

Be you, because no one else can be!

About the author

Kody Bateman is the Founder and CEO of SendOutCards, an international greeting card company that was featured in the 2009 Inc. 500 list as one of the fastest growing companies in the U.S. Kody is a visionary leader who is living his dream and travels the country teaching others to do the same.

He was born and raised in Salt Lake City, Utah, where he lives with his wife Jodi and his family. Kody first became a student of personal development at age sixteen when he read Dale Carnegie's book, *How to Win Friends and Influence People*. Since that time, he has wanted to be an influence for good in people's lives by helping them live positive and successful lives.

Kody received a bachelor's degree in marketing and started his career working for an advertising agency in New York. He returned to Utah after taking an executive marketing position with a food service company. In 1991, Kody was first exposed to network marketing. He embraced this unique business concept and has loved it ever since. In 1994, he started a telecommunications company that delivered services to network marketing companies and their distributors. With this business, Kody had a unique opportunity to learn from top executives and distributors from numerous network marketing companies. He has been working in the network marketing industry for over 15 years.

He has been a featured speaker at over 200 network marketing events in the past six years and has conducted personal development seminars for audiences all over the United States, Canada, and Australia.

Kody makes a point that the SendOutCards' movement is not about him: It is about every person who becomes a sender of cards. The story is only beginning to be written, and the true power of SendOutCards and its message lies in the tens of thousands of people who push the "send" button every day.

Kody does not believe that there is a "self-made" anybody. He believes we are all as good as the people around us. SendOutCards has attracted the most gifted people in the world. Because of this, the company is able to help others soar to the greatest heights possible.

One of Kody's stories tells about learning to rap on a street corner in Baltimore while serving a Christian mission for his church.

"When I rap, I am using my love of music and cherishing memories of people I love from the streets of Baltimore. Having fun with this rap music is a way for me to trigger the positive energy I had with those people, and it makes me feel good. It also celebrates the love of self and others," Kody says. To this day he carries a love for music, and has written and produced several inspirational songs and music videos. Kody is also an outdoor enthusiast. He competes in motocross and is a self-proclaimed "steep and deep" snowmobile rider.

Promptings: Your Inner Guide to Making a Difference

is also available as an eBook, as a CD set, or audio download.

Visit www.eagleonepublishing.com for details.

EAGLE ONE
PUBLISHING
PO Box 26173
Salt Lake City, UT 84126
www.eagleonepublishing.com